THE US ELECTION: A BASIC GUIDE

An essential guide for all those who've ever wanted to understand the system used to choose the most powerful leader in the Western world. With a detailed, but accessible approach, Michael Leapman explains the whole US election procedure. Suitable for the layperson as well as the student of US politics, this book traces the historical development of the US electoral system and then takes a close look at the policies and the candidates in the 1988 election. It makes entertaining, enlightening and invaluable reading.

About the author

Michael Leapman was born in London in 1938, and has been a journalist since he was 20. He worked for the *Scotsman* and the *Sun* before joining *The Times* as New York correspondent in 1969. He edited the paper's popular Diary column from 1972–1977 before travelling for another spell to New York. In 1981 he joined the *Daily Express* as a columnist and has been a freelance since 1983. He specialises in writing about media affairs, and has now produced six books. In 1983 he won the Thomas Cook Award for the best guidebook of 1983 for THE COMPANION GUIDE TO NEW YORK. His latest book, about the Labour leader Neil Kinnock, was published in 1987.

**Also by the same author
and available from Coronet:**

THE LAST DAYS OF THE BEEB

THE US ELECTION:
A BASIC GUIDE

Michael Leapman

CORONET BOOKS
Hodder and Stoughton

Copyright © 1988 by
Michael Leapman

First published in Great Britain
as a paperback original
in Coronet 1988

Printed and bound in Great Britain
for Hodder and Stoughton
Paperbacks, a division of Hodder
and Stoughton Limited, Mill Road,
Dunton Green, Sevenoaks, Kent.
TN13 2YA.
(Editorial Office: 47 Bedford
Square, London WC1B 3DP)
Photoset by Rowland
Phototypesetting Limited,
Bury St Edmunds, Suffolk.
Printed by Richard Clay Limited,
Bungay, Suffolk.

British Library C.I.P.

Leapman, Michael, *1938–*
   The U.S. election: a basic guide.
   1. United States. Presidents.
  Elections, 1988. Campaigns
  I. Title
  324.973'0927

   ISBN 0-340-42890-2

Contents

1 The American Presidency — 11

2 Post-War Presidents — 41

3 The Long Road to the White House — 74

4 The Political Map — 109

5 The Political System — 126

6 1988 – The Issues — 142

7 1988 – The Candidates — 153

8 Other 1988 Contests — 196

9 Sources — 201

   Index — 203

US PRESIDENTS AND VICE-PRESIDENTS

Elected		Party	Born	Served	Died	Vice-President
1788	George Washington	F	1732	1789–97	1799	John Adams
1796	John Adams	F	1735	1797–1801	1826	Thomas Jefferson
1800	Thomas Jefferson	DR	1743	1801–9	1826	Burr/Clinton
1808	James Madison	DR	1751	1809–17	1836	Clinton/Gerry
1816	James Monroe	DR	1758	1817–25	1831	Daniel Tompkins
1824	John Q. Adams	DR	1767	1825–29	1848	John Calhoun
1828	Andrew Jackson	D	1767	1829–37	1845	Calhoun/Van Buren
1836	Martin Van Buren	D	1782	1837–41	1862	Richard Johnson
1840	William H. Harrison	W	1773	3/41–4/41	1841	John Tyler
–	John Tyler	W	1790	1841–5	1862	–
1844	James Polk	D	1795	1845–9	1849	George Dallas
1848	Zachary Taylor	W	1784	1849–50	1850	Millard Fillmore
–	Millard Fillmore	W	1800	1850–3	1874	–
1852	Franklin Pierce	D	1804	1853–7	1869	William King
1856	James Buchanan	D	1791	1857–61	1868	John Breckinridge
1860	Abraham Lincoln	R	1809	1861–5*	1865	Hamlin/Johnson
–	Andrew Johnson	R	1808	1865–9	1875	–
1868	Ulysses S. Grant	R	1822	1869–77	1885	Colfax/Wilson
1876	Rutherford Hayes	R	1822	1877–81	1893	William Wheeler
1880	James Garfield	R	1831	3/81–9/81*	1891	Chester Arthur
–	Chester Arthur	R	1830	1881–5	1886	–

1884	Grover Cleveland	D	1885–9	1837	Thomas Hendricks	1908
1888	Benjamin Harrison	R	1889–93	1833	Levi Morton	1901
1892	Grover Cleveland	D	1893–7	1837	Adlai Stevenson	1908
1896	William McKinley	R	1897–1901*	1843	Hobart/Roosevelt	1901
1904	Theodore Roosevelt	R	1901–9	1858	Charles Fairbanks	1919
1908	William Taft	R	1909–13	1857	James Sherman	1930
1912	Woodrow Wilson	D	1913–21	1856	Thomas Marshall	1924
1920	Warren Harding	R	1921–3	1865	Calvin Coolidge	1923
1924	Calvin Coolidge	R	1923–9	1872	Charles Dawes	1933
1928	Herbert Hoover	R	1929–33	1874	Charles Curtis	1964
1932	Franklin Roosevelt	D	1933–45	1882	Garner/Wallace/Truman	1945
1948	Harry Truman	D	1945–53	1884	Alben Barkley	1972
1952	Dwight Eisenhower	R	1953–61	1890	Richard Nixon	1969
1960	John Kennedy	D	1961–3*	1917	Lyndon Johnson	1963
1964	Lyndon Johnson	D	1963–9	1908	Hubert Humphrey	1973
1968	Richard Nixon	R	1969–74†	1913	Agnew/Ford	
–	Gerald Ford	R	1974–7	1913	Nelson Rockefeller	
1976	Jimmy Carter	D	1977–81	1924	Walter Mondale	
1980	Ronald Reagan	R	1981–9	1911	George Bush	

D = Democrat, DR = Democratic Republican, F = Federalist, R = Republican, W = Whig

* = assassinated during term, † = resigned.

(Source: Congressional Quarterly)

1

The American Presidency

The chief reason why the Americans chose a presidential system of government was that the British did not have one. In 1787, eleven years after the thirteen American colonies formally broke their ties with Britain and declared themselves independent states, representatives of all of them (except Rhode Island, which disapproved of the proceeding) gathered in Independence Hall in Philadelphia to frame a constitution for their new nation. George III, King of England, symbolised the oppression, as they saw it, of more than a century of British rule, so they were unanimously opposed to duplicating the monarchy. There was no question, therefore, of making the head of state an hereditary office. Indeed, some delegates at the convention, notably Benjamin Franklin, thought that even an elected president would, like a king, too easily entrench himself and assume autocratic powers; they wanted executive authority to be vested in a council of representatives with no single head.

This view did not gain the day. James Wilson from Pennsylvania, an articulate Scot who later became a Supreme Court justice, argued that one man could most effectively carry out executive functions, because he could act more speedily than any committee in cases where swift decisions were needed. Thus Article 2 of the constitution agreed in Philadelphia states:

The executive power shall be vested in a President of the United States of America. He shall hold his office during the term of four years.

Article 1 concerned the apportionment of legislative powers to Congress. Putting the two articles in that order of precedence symboli⁻ed the determination of the framers that the executive should not hold sway over the legislature. In insisting on separating the two kinds of authority they were influenced by the French philosopher Montesquieu, who had written in 1748:

> When the legislative and executive powers are united in the same person, or in the same body of magistrates, there can be no liberty . . . Again, there is no liberty if the judiciary power be not separated from the legislative and executive.

That meant that as far as possible the makers of laws should be separate from those charged with putting them into effect and that the judiciary should have the power to review the actions of both. This was why, after a great deal of vacillation on the issue, the Convention decided that the President should not be chosen by Congress but elected separately, through an electoral college. This evolved in time into the form of popular election that exists today.

In the eleven years since they had declared independence and defeated the former colonisers in battle, the Americans had found that governing their new nation presented enormous difficulties. It had never in fact been a nation at all. The British had run the territory as thirteen separate colonies, each with its own governor who derived his authority direct from London. After the revolution the states simply replaced their separate colonial administrations with individual local authorities with wide autonomy, linked together only by a rough-and-ready federal system whose instrument was the Continental Congress.

The basis for this original union were the 'Articles of Confederation and Perpetual Union', adopted by the thirteen states in 1777. The union, perpetual or not, was built on a fragile structure. The Congress had limited powers over the states and an even more severely limited ability to impose its decisions. It could levy taxes but had no means of ensuring that they were paid, nor that the states fulfilled their obligation to provide men for the federal army. While the war of independence was still in progress, the co-operation engendered by a common struggle for survival had the effect of hiding these weaknesses. There was neither the time nor the incentive to revise the articles. But once the British withdrew in 1783 it was apparent that a system would have to be introduced that provided for a stronger central government.

George Washington, the hero of the war of independence, presided over the 1787 convention, attended by fifty-five delegates from twelve of the thirteen states. The extent of central authority as against the rights of the states was the point of principle underlying the long discussions, as it has underlain much political contention in America to the present day. The most fervent advocate of a strong central administration was Alexander Hamilton, the 32-year-old New York lawyer who was already one of the dominant intellects in the land.

Hamilton's advocacy of a powerful national government was viewed by representatives of the smaller states with deep suspicion. They feared that any central authority would be dominated by the more populous states, so that the interests of the smaller would suffer and their identity be buried. The solution, known as the Great Compromise, was to create a two-tier Congress in which the House of Representatives was composed of members elected by district in accordance with their population, while the upper house, the Senate, was made up of two senators from each state, regardless of its size. In return for that concession, the states forfeited the power to impose customs tariffs, mint their own coinage, enter into foreign treaties or raise armies without the approval of Congress.

The presidency, once accepted in principle, was clearly going to be a powerful instrument for imposing a unitary authority on reluctant states. Article 2 of the Constitution, after setting out in detail the 'college' method of conducting a presidential election, lists the powers and duties of the office holder, in this order:

Commander-in-chief of the US army and navy and of the states' militias when called into the service of the United States.

Power to seek reports in writing from heads of executive departments (the Cabinet).

Power to grant reprieves and pardons for offences against the USA, except in cases of impeachment.

With the advice and consent of the Senate, power to make treaties and appoint ambassadors, Supreme Court judges and other federal officials.

Power to fill vacancies in the Senate if they occur in mid-term.

Duty to report to Congress on the state of the union.

Power to recommend legislation to Congress.

Power to convene and adjourn the House of Representatives and the Senate in the event of disagreement between them. (This includes the significant power to call special sessions of Congress.)

Duty to receive ambassadors and to commission officers.

'He shall take care that the laws be faithfully executed.'

A further vitally important function is noted in Article 1 of the Constitution, in the section on passing bills and resolutions. This gives the President his 'veto power' to return any bill to the Congress without signing it. It then has to be passed by a two-thirds majority in both houses before it becomes law: otherwise it lapses. George Washington, the first President, used his veto power twice and it has been used many hundreds of times since, although often over-ridden by Congress.

The office of President, as devised by the 1787 Convention, is a unique and effective creation, combining the executive powers of a monarch with the function of a court of last resort on legislation. Working from no precedent, with no model available to copy from, the framers devised in the presidency an instrument of great strength.

It is probable, bearing in mind their detestation of the British monarchy, that they would have been stricter about limiting the powers of the office were it not for the (correct) assumption that the revered Washington would be its first holder and that he would exercise restraint in defining the limits of his authority. As it was, the immense power of this newly-created institution of government was not properly realised until Andrew Jackson's tenure from 1829 to 1837. What then prevented it from becoming an instrument of tyranny was the requirement that the holder should present himself for re-election every four years, even if the form of election was left unsatisfactorily vague.

The Electoral College

The method of electing the President was a subject of heated dispute at the Philadelphia Convention. Only a minority wanted it done by popular vote, which was not then a common means of selection for public office. Fears were expressed that even the strictly limited number of people then entrusted with the vote – essentially white male property owners, amounting to only about six per cent of American adults – were too unsophisticated to be entrusted with the task. It was felt that they would be too easily swayed by worthless promises and base their choice on qualities that, though superficially attractive, were not what was needed by the holder of the highest office in the land. Though they were in a mood to challenge many of the assumptions inherited from Britain, the concept of a ruling class was not among them. Alexander Hamilton wrote that the electors should be men 'most likely to possess the information and discernment requisite to such complicated investigations'.

The electoral system finally chosen was explained in great detail in the constitution, Article 2, Section 1:

Each state shall appoint, in such manner as the legislature thereof may direct, a number of electors, equal to the whole number of senators and representatives to which the state may be entitled in Congress: but no Senator or

Representative, or person holding an office of trust or profit under the United States, shall be appointed an elector.

The electors shall meet in their respective states, and vote by ballot for two persons, of whom one at least shall not be an inhabitant of the same state with themselves. And they shall make a list of all the persons voted for, and of the number of votes for each; which list they shall sign and certify, and transmit sealed to the seat of the Government of the United States, directed to the President of the Senate. The President of the Senate shall, in the presence of the Senate and the House of Representatives, open all the certificates and the votes shall then be counted.

The article goes on to explain what happens if there is no overall majority, when the election goes to the House of Representatives.

It was left to each state legislature to decide how to choose its electors. The initial assumption was that most would simply be appointed by the legislature, and this proved to be the case in the elections of 1788, 1792 and 1796. But as the nineteenth century dawned, a broader concept of democracy began to take root and states gradually went over to a system of popular votes, until by 1832 only South Carolina was sticking to the old formula.

No matter how they were chosen, by the last years of the eighteenth century the members of the electoral college had ceased to exercise any independent judgment on the matter of who should be President, but were there simply to represent the political party in whose name they had been elected.

The Party System

There were no formal political parties in the United States at the time of the Philadelphia Convention, and they are not mentioned in the Constitution. Some of the framers hoped, a little naively, that they would never be created, that democracy could be conducted on the basis of the collective wisdom of reasonable men, responsive to the views of the citizens who elected them. That worked, up to a point, during the presidency of George Washington, a figure who stood above party divisions and who indeed deplored the very idea of them. At the completion of his second term in 1796 he decided not to run for a third. Factions were already grouping around the contenders for the succession, and in his farewell address Washington warned his audience about the danger, as he saw it, of giving rein to party rivalry:

> It serves always to distract the public councils and enfeeble the public administration. It agitates the community with ill-founded jealousies and false alarms; kindles the animosity of one part against another; foments occasionally riot and insurrection.

These strictures were never likely to be heeded. Divisions had already emerged in Washington's cabinet between the Federalists, supporters of Alexander Hamilton's advocacy of a powerful central government, and Thomas Jefferson's Republicans, who wanted more autonomy for the states. (The latter party was later known as the Democratic or Jeffersonian Republicans and, confusingly, is the forerunner of today's Democratic Party, not Republican.)

It has never been easy to define American political parties by the conventional left/right criteria that apply in Europe, but the Federalists were the more conservative of the two. Hamilton was a conscious supporter of rule by a monied elite – a group whose position he strengthened when he created the Bank of the United States as the central financial institution of the new country. He was among those who took the view that the common people were unqualified to make rational choices from among the contenders for leadership. Jefferson, on the other hand, was suspicious of any institution that seemed to place more power in the hands of the Federal government. That is why the main support for Jefferson came from the southern states, always opposed to the accretion of power at the centre.

In 1792, though, the only question about the presidency had been whether Washington could be persuaded to stand for a second term. Once he agreed, his election was automatic. That did not, however, apply to the vice-presidency. Hamilton, the Secretary of the Treasury, backed the incumbent, John Adams. Jefferson, Secretary of State, campaigned for Governor George Clinton of New York. This was the first real manifestation of party politics in a United States presidential election. It resulted in a win for Adams and the Federalists, by seventy-seven electoral college votes to fifty.

Four years later, when Washington stood down (partly because of his dismay at the growth of factional politics), Hamilton's party repeated its success in the vote for President, with Adams defeating Jefferson – but by the narrow margin of seventy-one votes to sixty-eight. Jefferson, by virtue of coming second, became Vice-President. The result showed that strict party voting had not yet become the norm. With each elector having two votes, it should have been possible to elect the 'ticket' of Adams and his running mate Thomas Pinckney into the first two positions, but only fifty-nine of those who voted for Adams supported his running mate as well.

By the time of the next election, in 1800, party discipline had taken effect. This time the Republicans triumphed, with Jefferson and his running mate Aaron Burr gaining seventy-three votes, Adams sixty-five and C. C. Pinckney (Thomas Pinckney's brother) sixty-four. This made a nonsense of the procedure envisaged by the constitution under which each member of the electoral college would vote for his first and second choices, the winner being President and the runner-up Vice-President. Now that the electors were chosen for their party affiliations, they would automatically vote for their party ticket, so both the candidates of any one party would receive the same number of votes and the election would always have to be decided in the House of Representatives.

On this occasion, the House chose Jefferson after thirty-six ballots.

In recognition of the political reality, and to avoid such an outcome in future, the constitution was amended before the 1804 election to allow separate ballots for President and Vice-President. Jefferson won a second term comfortably, with 162 votes to C. C. Pinckney's fourteen. By now seven of the seventeen states were choosing their electoral college representatives by popular vote, three by a district system and seven by appointment by state legislatures.

The Federalists never wholly recovered from that crushing defeat. (Hamilton, their leader, had been killed by Aaron Burr in a duel not long before the presidential election.) They retained support in New England but scarcely anywhere else. In 1808 C. C. Pinckney improved his showing with forty-seven votes, but that came nowhere near James Madison's 122.

The Madison presidency was notable for the role played by his wife Dolley, the first of the assertive First Ladies who recognised and exploited the potential of her position to wield a powerful influence on affairs of state. After leaving the White House, she remained a popular Washington hostess until her death in 1849 at the age of eighty-one.

Madison won again in 1812, although by a narrower margin. The Federalists had now lost four elections in a row and could see no prospect of turning the tide. Some spoke of organising the secession of the New England states from the union, and when the British launched an attack in 1812, trying to retake their former colonies, there were Federalists who wanted to make a separate peace in the north-east. The defeat of the British at New Orleans in 1815 (although not before they had raided Washington and burned the White House) meant the effective end of the Federalist party. In 1816 it contested its last election, when Rufus King could muster only thirty-four votes against James Monroe's 183. Four years later two Republicans ran and Monroe won all but one of the 232 college votes against his Secretary of State, John Quincy Adams.

Monroe's lasting contribution to American statecraft was the Monroe Doctrine contained in his message to Congress in 1823. The former Spanish colonies in South and Central America had just won their independence but there were fears that Spain or one of the other European powers would try to regain control of them. Monroe declared that the United States would not countenance any further attempts at colonisation or interference by Europeans in its hemisphere – a doctrine that has survived and helps explain United States concern over events in Cuba in 1962 and in Nicaragua more recently.

John Quincy Adams played an influential role in drafting the doctrine and was rewarded by victory in the 1824 presidential election in a bitterly fought contest in which all four candidates were Republicans. None achieved an overall majority and the House of Representatives chose Adams, even though Andrew Jackson, 'Old Hickory', hero of the war against Britain, had won the largest number of votes in the electoral college. As a result of this clear distortion of the will of the electorate, and the bitterness surrounding it, the Republican Party split into pro-Adams and pro-Jackson factions. The Jackson supporters came to be known as the Democratic Republicans, later simply the Democratic Party. The Adams group were the National Republicans.

Another consequence of the 1824 result was to intensify pressure to democratise the system of choosing electors. By 1828 all but two states – South Carolina and Delaware – were selecting their electoral college delegates by some form of popular vote. The number of men able to vote that year was three times higher than in 1824.

Jackson easily won the 1828 election, partly because of his justifiable claim that he had been cheated out of the presidency four years earlier. He is often regarded as the first popularly elected President and was certainly the first not to be part of the Eastern establishment – he came from what was then the south-western frontier in Tennessee. He was also the first to adopt the now widely accepted practice of removing the previous administration's appointees from senior government positions and replacing them with his own supporters. To this day patronage – it was then called the 'spoils system' – remains a powerful element in American party politics. In a message to Congress, Jackson delivered a vigorous defence of the practice of replacing office-holders regularly and ruthlessly:

> There are, perhaps, few men who can for any length of time enjoy office and power without being more or less under the influence of feelings unfavourable to the faithful discharge of their public duties . . . Office is considered as a species of property, and government rather as a means of promoting individual interests than as an instrument created solely for the service of the people.

He was the first President to create a 'kitchen cabinet' of trusted advisers who would exert an important influence on policy even though they held no formal government position.

Jackson developed many of the powers of the modern presidency, gathering greater authority to the White House than any of his predecessors. In doing so he downgraded the role of Congress in the executive branch of government. He also stood firm against attempts by states to override decisions of his administration, notably when South Carolina sought to opt out of a new tariff that protected the industries of the northern states at the expense of the south. Jackson threatened to use force to compel the state to comply. South Carolina backed down, but the issue of states' rights continued to be critical and would lead eventually to the Civil War.

The system takes shape

One of the most characteristic and enduring institutions of American politics came into being in Philadelphia in 1830 when the Anti-Masonic party – a transient but quite influential group later subsumed by the Whigs – held the first

national convention to select their candidates for office.
Two years later the Democrats followed suit in Baltimore.
Previously, candidates had risen naturally to the top of
Washington's power elite, as cream rises in milk – a similar
process to that by which leaders of the British Conservative
Party used to 'emerge'. In effect, this had meant that no
candidate could be nominated without the approval of Congress – an arrangement in conflict with the principle of
separation of powers that was one of the most important
features of the constitution. With the growth of real democracy a more open system of selection was needed. The idea
that candidates should be chosen by rank and file members,
delegated by their local state parties, was in accord with the
spirit of the times. The noisy and colourful displays of support
for individual candidates at the conventions, combined with
power broking behind the scenes, have down the years come
to symbolise the American political system (see pages 96 to
98).

Those who resented Jackson's move towards a more
powerful presidency, including the Anti-Masons and the
rump of the National Republicans, formed a new party, the
Whigs. In 1836 two candidates contested the presidential
election under the Whig banner – William Harrison and
Daniel Webster. Both were defeated by the Democrat,
Martin Van Buren. In 1839 the Whigs, at their first convention, chose Harrison as their candidate. He beat Van
Buren in the 1840 election, bringing to an end forty years of
rule by the Democrats and their immediate forebears.

With the nominating process now opened out to the common people, it was time for the election itself to become a
popular national event. The 1840 campaign saw the introduction of publicity techniques that endured for a century, until
modern communications – specifically television – made
many of them redundant. Harrison and John Tyler, his
vice-presidential running-mate, travelled across the country
and held exuberant political meetings, with rousing music and
razzamatazz, free cider, colourful campaign literature and
even badges. Harrison's purpose was to promote a vigorous

image of himself as a simple outdoorsman, most at home in a
log cabin, and a war hero in the mould of Andrew Jackson.
He had led the federal army to a famous victory against the
Indians at Tippecanoe in 1811. He dubbed himself 'Old Tip'
and coined one of the first campaign slogans in American
history: 'Tippecanoe and Tyler too.'

His campaign songs showed a nice touch of venom, as:

> Old Tip he wears a homespun suit,
> He has no ruffled shirt-wirt-wirt;
> But Mat he has the golden plate,
> And he's a little squirt-wirt-wirt.

The last line was often followed by a demonstrative spit.

These efforts assured Harrison of a convincing victory in
the electoral college, by 234 votes to sixty. The popular vote
was much closer, 1,275,000 to 1,129,000, showing how the
college could misrepresent true opinion.

One purpose of Harrison's energetic campaign had been to
show he was in the best of health and to counter the 'age
issue': he was sixty-seven. Ironically, he died a month after his
inauguration in 1841 – the first President to die in office.

Tyler served the rest of the term, but it was not a happy one.
He fell out with Henry Clay of Kentucky, the Whig leader in
the Senate and the effective leader of the party, and vetoed
two attempts by members of his own party to re-establish a
national bank. Tyler, unlike the majority of Whigs, was a
'strict constructionist' (see page 137). He believed the
Federal Government's powers had to be restricted to those
stated in the Constitution – which did not include the establishment of a national bank. That view was prevalent in the
southern states. The opposite doctrine was that the government was entitled to assume additional 'implied powers' that
were within the spirit of the Constitution if not its letter.

So angry were his Whig colleagues with Tyler's leadership
that his entire Cabinet resigned in 1841. Some members of his
party wanted him impeached – the only way Congress can call
a President to account. But since the Constitution allows

impeachment only for 'treason, bribery or other high crimes or misdemeanours', the attempt was abandoned. Before the 1844 election Tyler made approaches to the Democrats, inquiring whether he might get their nomination; but it went to James Polk, who defeated the Whig Henry Clay.

The second and last Whig President was Zachary Taylor, a former soldier with notable victories against Indians to his credit. He was elected in 1848 but died in 1850, when he was succeeded by the Vice-President, Millard Fillmore. By this time, the apparatus of the modern presidency and the machinery for elections to it were established. It had taken some sixty years, a very brief period compared with the time other countries have taken to create their institutions of government. Except for the fact that one of today's two major political parties had yet to be formed, a time traveller from the mid-nineteenth century would find little changed in the American system as it operates in 1988.

Civil War, assassination and impeachment

Over the next decade the issue that came to dominate American politics was the right to keep slaves. Broadly, the Northern states opposed it while the south was determined to retain the right, pointing out that the Constitution did not bar it, for it had nothing to say on the question. The Whigs, whose main power was in the north-east but who enjoyed sectional support in the south, took no stand on slavery. The Democratic majority in the south were in favour of it, but not the party's supporters in the north. In 1854 a new party, the Republicans, was formed in unequivocal opposition to the slave system. Their first presidential candidate, John Fremont, came a respectable second to the Democrat James Buchanan in 1856, with 114 college votes to the winner's 174. For the fading Whigs, Millard Fillmore could muster only eight.

During Buchanan's presidency, the seeds of the Civil War were sown. Just after his inauguration in 1857, the Supreme

Court delivered its notorious 'Dred Scott decision', to the effect that Congress had no power to legislate over slavery and the states had to decide for themselves whether to allow it. Most of the Supreme Court justices held slaves. Buchanan supported the decision but northern Democrats deplored it and formed a breakaway party. In 1860 its candidate won more votes than the southern Democrat, but the split gave the Republicans their first presidential victor, in the redoubtable person of Abraham Lincoln. (He won a majority in the electoral college even though he gained only forty per cent of the popular vote in a four-cornered contest.)

In 1861, the year Lincoln took office, eleven southern states broke away from the Union and formed the Confederacy. When rebels fired on Fort Sumter in South Carolina, Lincoln called for troops and the Civil War was under way. The war was still in progress at the time of the next presidential election, although victory for the Union was by then certain. Lincoln stood for the National Union Party: in effect the Republicans under a new patriotic name that did not last much longer than the war. He won the election easily but served little of his second term, for he was assassinated at a theatre in Washington two weeks before the surrender of the southern armies. The first US President to be assassinated was succeeded by Andrew Johnson, the first – and so far the only – US President to be impeached.

Johnson was a stubborn southerner, who had represented Tennessee in the Senate but had refused to recognise the state's secession in 1861. As President, he fulfilled the spirit of Lincoln's second inaugural address ('With malice toward none . . . let us bind up the nation's wounds') by granting pardons to nearly everyone involved in the Confederate cause. The southern states ratified the Thirteenth Amendment to the constitution, which read:

Neither slavery nor involuntary servitude, except as a punishment for crime whereof the party shall have been duly convicted, shall exist within the United States, or any place subject to their jurisdiction.

But the 'radical' northern majority in Congress wanted to exert tougher conditions on the re-admission of the southern states than Johnson did, including large-scale confiscation of the property of the former rebels. One reason for this was practical: the emancipation of the slaves meant that the population figure for the southern states, on which Congressional representation was based, increased significantly, allowing them twenty-nine extra seats. But although counted as citizens for that purpose, the negroes would not be allowed the vote. The result would be that the extra seats would nearly all be filled by Democrats, threatening the Republican majority.

The difference of opinion between Congress and the President resulted in the most serious clash between the executive and the legislature in the country's ninety-year history. Johnson vetoed bills imposing tough terms on 'reconstruction' for the south, because he thought they infringed states' rights; but his veto was over-ridden. Congress also passed the Tenure of Office Act, forbidding the President to remove officials he had appointed unless the Senate gave its approval – a serious curtailment of presidential prerogatives.

That Act was the trigger for the impeachment. Edwin Stanton, appointed by Lincoln as Secretary for War, was among Johnson's leading critics and in February 1868 the President dismissed him, ignoring the Senate's objections. He was impeached for that and other alleged misdemeanours. After a 'trial' in the Senate, which he declined to attend, he was saved by a single vote. For impeachment to succeed, his accusers needed a two-thirds majority – thirty-six of the fifty-four senators. Had the vote gone along party lines he would have been doomed, for there were forty-two Republicans in the Senate. (Johnson was technically a Republican but he was no longer accepted as such by most party members.) But seven Republicans joined the twelve Democrats to allow him to survive. Although the affair had destroyed Johnson's personal prospects of re-election, the failure by Congress to remove him from office had the effect of restoring the balance of power between the executive and the legislature, which had tipped decisively towards the legislature during his presidency. Impeachment has been threatened on occasion since – most recently in the case of President Nixon – but it has not gone ahead.

Soldiers and scandals

The first President of the United States was a war hero and that set a precedent for many of his successors. One of the few countries in the world that has never been subjected to a military dictatorship, the United States often gives its supreme office voluntarily to men who have shown their worth – and, more important, established their identity with the voters – on the battlefield. Andrew Jackson, William Harrison and Zachary Taylor were three, all serving in the second quarter of the nineteenth century.

General Ulysses S. Grant was the fifth soldier President and, after Washington, the most distinguished, at least militarily. He fought in the Mexican War of 1846–8 but left the army in 1854, partly on account of his immoderate drinking. When the Civil War began he was called back to the colours in his home state of Illinois, with the rank of brigadier-general. After two victories there he was made a major-general and led the Union troops to important victories. In 1864 he was placed in command of the whole army and given the task of securing the final victory. That came a year later when he accepted General Lee's surrender at Appomattox. In 1866 he was created the first full general since Washington and served briefly under Johnson as Secretary for War after the dismissal of Stanton. He was clearly going to be a valuable asset to the political party that secured him as a presidential candidate. In 1868 he quit Johnson's Cabinet and was nominated by the Republicans. He won two elections – the first two in which black Americans were allowed to vote – and wanted to defy tradition by going for a third.

Grant's presidency was less distinguished than his generalship, tainted as it was with scandal. Since Andrew Jackson introduced the practice of making political appointments to top federal jobs, the first few months of a presidency saw the arrival in Washington of scores of supplicants seeking positions. Because Grant had no background in politics, the people he surrounded himself with were not, for the most part, politicians, but friends and relatives.

One of them, his brother-in-law, became involved with two New York financiers, Jay Gould and Jim Fisk, who had launched an improbable scheme to corner the market in gold. It was a corrupt era and the turbulence of the Civil War had caused instability in the young nation's institutions. The machinations of 'Boss Tweed' on the municipal administration in New York were about to be exposed. The success of Fisk and Gould's scheme depended upon the Treasury refusing to release extra supplies of gold from the federal reserve, for in the event of such a release the value of their holdings would plummet. They had been told by Grant's brother-in-law that no new gold would be released, although how far the President had been consulted is unclear. When extra supplies of gold *were* released the price duly dropped and thousands of investors were bankrupted, although Gould and Fisk, forewarned, sold their holdings just in time.

In 1873, as Grant's second term began, a financial panic heralded a long-term depression. Numerous members of his administration were caught up in scandals and some were made to resign. Only his war record, and the respect in which he was still held for it, prevented a total collapse of public support; although that did not deter him from an attempt to get himself nominated for an unprecedented third term. By a convincing margin, however, Congress declared him ineligible to run.

In the aftermath of the scandals, the Republicans lost control of the House of Representatives in the mid-term elections, heralding six years of clashes between the executive and the legislature. Nor did it appear likely that the Republicans would hold the White House in 1876. In the event they did, but only narrowly and in highly suspect circumstances. It was not a vintage election in terms of the candidates. Neither

Rutherford Hayes, the Republican Governor of Ohio, nor Samuel Tilden, Democratic Governor of New York, could boast a charismatic personality. But what the campaign lacked in excitement the count made up for. Allegations of electoral fraud and corruption, some of them well-based, were bandied between the parties, particularly in the marginal southern states, where the votes of white Democrats had been offset by those of newly enfranchised blacks.

Hayes was declared the winner by a single electoral college vote, 185 to 184, although there was no doubt that Tilden had won the majority of the popular vote, with 4,285,992 to Hayes' 4,033,768. The Democrats did not accept the result of the vote for college electors in four states – Florida, Louisiana, Oregon and South Carolina. An electoral commission was established to rule on the dispute, composed of five senators, five representatives and five Supreme Court justices. They decided for Hayes. The Democrats agreed to accept the verdict after negotiating a deal in which the new President promised to end the political power of the 'carpetbaggers', northerners who had gone to the defeated southern states after the Civil War and exercised power corruptly.

The era of dark horses

The Hayes presidency marked the start of a sequence of undistinguished holders of the office. This was to a large extent due to the convention system of selecting candidates. Both main national parties have always been coalitions of groups with differing views. At convention time each faction would have its own favourite for the nomination. After numerous ballots, the choice would normally fall on somebody who scored low in the original ballots but whose personality was not sufficiently assertive to have antagonised any of the main factions. Hayes had been a compromise between the magnetic James Blaine, Speaker of the House of Representatives and an advocate of continued tough measures.

against the renegade south; and Benjamin Bristow, the reformist Secretary of the Treasury.

In 1880 the man who eventually became the Republican candidate, and then the President, did not figure at all in the early rounds of voting at the convention. Delegates were at first broadly divided between three candidates: Blaine again; Grant, still trying for his third term after a spell travelling abroad; and John Sherman, Secretary of the Treasury. James Garfield had managed Sherman's campaign and was also a friend of Blaine, so he had good credentials as the least objectionable to the greatest number of people. Because of his role in the Sherman campaign, Garfield was at the convention when he was nominated – the first to break the tradition that candidates absent themselves from the proceedings.

Garfield was in office for less than a year before becoming the second US President to fall victim to an assassin. His successor was the Vice-President, Chester Arthur, who four years earlier had been dismissed as customs commissioner in New York following allegations of corruption. Arthur had been put on the ticket to appease the 'stalwart' or conservative wing of the party, who had disapproved of the nomination of the reformer Garfield. The fact that the makeweight succeeded to the highest office demonstrated the hazards of the 'balanced ticket' – as Andrew Johnson, Lincoln's Vice-President, had shown two decades earlier. With a pair of candidates chosen to appeal to the broadest spectrum of the electorate, the qualities of the vice-presidential nominee are likely to be the opposite of those of the man who heads the ticket. So if the second man does succeed to the presidency, the country gets the reverse of what it voted for.

Arthur's effectiveness as President was marred by hostility from the reform element of his own party and, for the second half of his term, from a Democratic majority of Congress. In 1884 the Republicans did not nominate him for a second term, preferring the veteran Blaine. So long the king-maker, Blaine was destined not to be king, for he was narrowly defeated in the election by the Democrat, Grover Cleveland, comparatively unknown until being elected Governor of New York two years earlier and tackling the corrupt Tammany Hall influence over the state's politics.

Cleveland won despite having to endure an early version of the sexual scandals that have dogged many modern contenders for the presidency. The press revealed – and he subsequently confessed – that ten years earlier he had fathered an illegitimate son, by a woman with a lurid reputation. That set the tone for a campaign steeped in personal innuendoes. Supporters of Blaine devised a cruel chant:

Ma, Ma, where's my pa? Gone to the White House, ha, ha, ha.

Democrats countered with:

Blaine, Blaine, James G. Blaine, the Continental liar from the state of Maine.

At the end of all the mud-slinging, Cleveland became the first Democratic President since the Civil War. It was a tribute to the tenacity of the party that it could come back after those long years in the wilderness.

Cleveland's term of office was notable in constitutional terms for his unrestrained use of the presidential veto. His twenty-one predecessors, in the ninety-six years of the presidency before he took office, had used the veto 132 times. Cleveland, in his first term, cast 413 vetoes, chiefly in pursuit of his opposition to federal patronage. Congressmen would take advantage of the fact that the federal budget was then substantially in surplus, and introduce bills to provide their constituents with federal benefits, primarily Civil War pensions. Cleveland believed this to be a corruption of the system and he would not sign such bills. His veto rate remained unchallenged for fifty years, until Franklin Roosevelt became equally insistent on getting his way with Congress.

Cleveland's antipathy to patronage also persuaded him to resist the demands of his party for extensive appointments to government positions. As the first Democrat in the White

House for twenty-eight years, he was under pressure to allot 'jobs for the boys'. Although he complied in some cases, he refused to engage in the wholesale change in personnel that was being urged on him, recognising that it was a recipe for administrative chaos.

The party nominated Cleveland again in 1888, but he lost the election despite winning more popular votes than his Republican rival, Benjamin Harrison. A grandson of the ninth President, William Henry Harrison, his term of office was chiefly notable for the addition of six north-western states to the union, bringing the total to forty-four.

In 1892 the choice reverted to Cleveland, the first President to be re-elected for a non-consecutive term. His second administration was dogged by financial crises, sparked by the panic of 1893. It was, too, an era when organised labour was beginning to flex its muscles. Cleveland sent 2,000 federal troops to Chicago to break a strike by Pullman car workers on the railway, led by one of the pioneers of American socialism, Eugene Debs – later a frequent third-party presidential candidate.

The Republicans were able to use the 'red scare' in the 1896 election, which pitted their candidate, William McKinley, against the charismatic 36-year-old William Jennings Bryan, who had won the support of a number of left-inclined groups (notably the small but noisy Populist party) as well as the nomination of the Democrats. Bryan had secured the nomination through an electrifying speech at the Democratic convention in Chicago, in support of minting a silver currency and retreating from the gold standard. This was the key political issue of the day. Wealthy businessmen and manufacturers supported the gold standard and high tariff barriers, while a silver coinage was seen as favouring the poor and the farmers. Bryan's performance in Chicago was known as the 'cross of gold' speech. It contained this memorable plea against the gold standard:

> You shall not press down upon the brow of labour this crown of thorns, you shall not crucify mankind upon a cross of gold.

This gained him an instant reputation for oratory and his campaign meetings drew large crowds. But much of the Eastern press came out against him, even those newspapers that normally supported the Democrats. Cartoonists linked him with Debs and other figures from the left, and McKinley won quite easily.

Looking outwards

McKinley's term of office was dominated by overseas issues, specifically the Spanish-American war. The Cubans had rebelled against their Spanish colonisers in the last year of Cleveland's presidency, but the Democrat had stood out against intervention. McKinley, under strong public pressure from the newspaper magnate William Randolph Hearst, threatened Spain with retaliation if it did not withdraw its forces from the island. The war lasted only a few months during 1898. As a result of it, Cuba became independent but with strong American links, and Spain ceded the Philippines, Puerto Rico and Guam to the United States. Entering the twentieth century, the republic, for the first time, was making its presence felt on the international scene.

A war is usually an electoral asset. The election of 1900 was contested by the same two candidates as four years earlier. Bryan took an anti-imperialist line and opposed the acquisition of the Spanish territories, but this did not accord with public sentiment and he lost more decisively than in 1896.

Another feature of the 1900 election was the energetic role of the Republican vice-presidential candidate, Theodore Roosevelt. The colourful military hero of the war against Spain, elected Governor of New York in 1898, made more impact on the campaign trail than McKinley himself. Those who marked him down as a future President were proved right sooner than they had anticipated. McKinley became yet another assassination victim in September 1901, six months after his second inauguration. He was shot by an anarchist while visiting an exhibition in Buffalo, New York.

At forty-two, Roosevelt became the youngest President in American history and one of the most popular. His energy and lack of pomp reflected the mood of a nation on the verge of the technological revolution that was to transform it into the most powerful country in the world. His most lasting achievement was the Panama Canal, begun during his term of office, although he had to foment a revolution in Panama to get it under way. His tough line with big business interests and his concern for conservation reinforced his popularity and there was never much doubt that he would win convincingly in 1904. Although there was then no law against a third term, he declared, as soon as he was announced the winner in 1904, that he would not run in 1908. Instead his protégé, William Howard Taft, a former governor of the Philippines and Secretary for War, was nominated by the Republicans and defeated Bryan, back for a third try. (Bryan remained active in politics but was never again a candidate for the highest office. In later years he became known for his vociferous opposition to Charles Darwin's theory of evolution and its teaching in American schools.)

Taft successfully continued his predecessor's battle against the large corporate trusts. In 1912, however, Roosevelt sought his party's nomination to return to the White House. Taft was unwilling to stand down and a bitter selection battle took place. By now, primary elections were beginning to be used in some states as a means of selecting delegates to the party conventions. Primaries had been introduced in Florida in 1901, then in Wisconsin, as a means of choosing candidates for state offices. They quickly caught on and by 1912 twelve states chose their delegates to national conventions through direct election at primaries, rather than in closed party gatherings as before.

In those twelve states Roosevelt won overwhelmingly. In

the others, though, Taft now had a firm grip on the party machine, including the ability to ensure that his supporters kept their jobs with the federal administration. At a fiercely contested convention in Chicago, amid allegations of trickery from Roosevelt's supporters, Taft won the nomination. A stubborn Roosevelt ran as the candidate of a new party, the Progressives. It was clear that the pair would split the anti-Democratic vote and render a Democratic victory almost certain – but the Democrats themselves were equally divided. They spent seven days in Baltimore agreeing on a candidate and eventually chose Woodrow Wilson, Governor of New Jersey, former President of Princeton University and son of a Presbyterian minister. In the election Roosevelt gained more votes than Taft, but Wilson, with only forty-two per cent of the popular vote, became the first Democratic President for sixteen years.

World War One began in the middle of Wilson's first term. He supported the British and their allies but, because of the large number of Americans whose roots were in Germany, he sought to keep out of any formal participation. Americans had historically been disinclined to get involved in European disputes. The sinking in 1915 of the liner *Lusitania*, whose passengers included 128 Americans, struck a blow at that traditional isolationism but Wilson was able to fight and just win the 1916 election using the slogan: 'He kept us out of war'. That aphorism held good only for a few months after he began his second term in 1917, when the United States formally joined the war on the Allied side. It was an unpopular commitment and in the mid-term elections the following year the Democrats lost control of Congress.

Wilson's reputation was largely ruined by his role at the Versailles peace conference in 1919. Many felt that he had compromised the dignity of his office by going at all, but more were dubious about the plan to form a League of Nations to reduce the chance of future world conflict. Wilson initialled the treaty – indeed the League had been his idea – but it was repudiated by Congress, who objected in particular to the clause pledging member nations to go to the aid of others if attacked. They believed this interfered with the war-making powers of Congress.

Although a majority in both houses voted for ratification, the margin did not reach the necessary two-thirds. Isolationism won the day. Wilson was discredited politically and now destroyed physically, too. On a national tour to drum up support for the treaty, he collapsed with a stroke and never recovered. He was physically unable to be more than a token leader during his final year as President. His wife Edith stepped in to insulate him from the strains of office and, said some, to assume many of its powers herself. Certainly she was the most assertive First Lady to have occupied the White House since Dolley Madison more than 100 years earlier.

Corruption and depression

The Democrats could not possibly win the 1920 election after the Wilson debacle, but the Republicans were unable to find a strong candidate to take the fullest advantage of their opponents' disarray. Theodore Roosevelt had died the previous year. The choice fell on Warren Harding, a senator from Ohio of no more than average prominence. In desperation, some Democrats tried the smear tactics that had by now become a familiar part of the election scene, suggesting that Harding had negro blood in his ancestry. Despite that the Republican won by a landslide. The election was notable for two innovations: it was the first in which women were allowed to vote, and the first in which a systematic attempt was made to take a public opinion poll during the campaign. A periodical called the *Literary Digest* sent out eleven million postcards and used them as the basis of predicting the Republican victory that had in any case been widely assumed.

Another sign of the times: Harding's inauguration was transmitted live on the increasingly popular medium of radio. His actual administration, however, was short on achievement and was destined to be curtailed as well: he died in August 1923 in an hotel in San Francisco. The official cause was bronchial pneumonia but there were persistent rumours of suicide or murder. They were inspired not by any hard evidence, but by well-founded tales of corruption in his administration, the extent of which emerged in full only after his death. The most notorious was the Teapot Dome scandal.

Teapot Dome is an area near Casper, Wyoming, that in 1915 had been ceded to the US Navy as an oil reserve, along with another extensive reserve at Elk Hills, California. In 1921 responsibility for the two areas was quietly transferred to the Department of the Interior. Soon after Harding's death it emerged that his Secretary of the Interior, Albert Fall, had leased the reserves to two large oil producers. In return for the favour, the oil men had set up a dummy corporation that passed cash and bonds to Fall and to the Republican National Committee. Fall quickly resigned and was eventually convicted; but investigations into the scandal spilled over to involve other members of the administration. The Attorney General and Secretary of the Navy resigned under pressure.

It fell to Calvin Coolidge, the Vice-President who had succeeded to the presidency, to untangle the scandal. Against the odds, he managed to keep his reputation unsullied, and won the 1924 election easily. This was partly because the country was going through a period of post-war prosperity and partly because of a deep split between southern and northern Democrats on issues such as black rights and liquor prohibition (which had come into force in 1920, after a constitutional amendment). The Democrats' convention in New York had been the longest in history, needing 103 ballots over fifteen days before John Davis was selected as the candidate.

Coolidge played a low-key role as the nation progressed to apparently limitless wealth. The main surprise of his term was his announcement in 1927 that he would not seek re-election. He never explained his reason, although he was upset by the death of a son and worried about his own health. In the 1928 election Herbert Hoover, the former mining engineer from Iowa who became Secretary of Commerce, continued the run

of comfortable Republican victories, this time against Alfred
E. Smith, the Democratic Governor of New York.

Hoover was the first President born west of the Mississippi
but he was not destined to be remembered for that. In 1929,
the year of his inauguration, came the Wall Street crash,
followed by the great depression. Hoover insisted at first that
no executive action was needed and that matters would soon
improve – much the same message as President Reagan
conveyed after the crash of 1987. When things only grew
worse, the administration tried some palliative measures such
as public works programmes, but they were more or less
ineffective. All the same, the Republicans nominated Hoover
to fight again in 1932, when he was pitted against Franklin
Delano Roosevelt, a relative of the former President. In the
circumstances, with the total of unemployed approaching
fifteen million, it was an unequal fight.

New Deal

In his speech accepting nomination at the Chicago convention, Roosevelt used the phrase 'new deal' to describe what he
had in mind for the hard-pressed American people. This has
become the accepted description of the first half of his unpre-
cedentedly long term of office. He reversed Hoover's *laissez-
faire* attitude and instituted a wide range of social policies
designed to protect Americans from the worst effects of a
harsh economic climate. His 'fireside chats' on the radio,
explaining his measures, created a new intimacy between the
President and the people that heralded a long-term change in
the public perception of the office.

In forcing through Congress the landmark legislation of his
first hundred days, Roosevelt used the presidential powers as
they had never been used before. His first executive act was to
close the banks while he called Congress to an emergency
session to pass a bill regulating banking. A stream of further
legislation was drafted in the White House and passed by
Congress, giving the President the authority to control prices

and government salaries and to initiate comprehensive relief and social security programmes. America went off the gold standard. Regulatory authorities were established for the stock markets and deposit-taking institutions.

Americans have seldom taken kindly to regulation but the economy was in such poor shape that they welcomed any positive measures that might help improve things. In the 1936 election, the Republicans – aided by a friendly press – attempted to characterise the New Deal as the product of an overbearing administration, inclined towards socialism, threatening traditional liberties; but their campaign fell flat. In an unequalled landslide, the President won 523 of the 531 electoral college votes against the hapless Republican, Alf Landon. And the Democrats enjoyed huge majorities in both houses of Congress.

The second Roosevelt term was less felicitous than the first. The Supreme Court had declared some New Deal legislation unconstitutional. To moderate the Court's conservative temper, the President sought to appoint extra justices, but Congress, despite its Democratic majority, would not let him. And a recession in the first year of the new term raised doubts about the long-lasting efficacy of his measures.

All this seemed less relevant when World War Two broke out in 1939. The United States was firmly committed to the British cause from the outset and would probably soon enter the war, as it had done in 1917. The sense of emergency put the nation in a mood to endorse the breaking of a tradition as old as the Republic: that no President should present himself for election for a third time. It was then only a tradition, not enshrined in the constitution. But with an external threat imminent, it was natural that people should want to stick with a tried leader. Roosevelt therefore ran again in 1940 and again won decisively, this time trouncing Wendell Wilkie. Once more, he triumphed despite a largely hostile press.

The United States joined the war after the Japanese bombed Pearl Harbor in December 1941. At the time of the next election, in 1944, peace was still many months away. Thomas Dewey, the Republican Governor of New York, put up a better show than Roosevelt's other victims, gaining 45.9 per cent of the vote, but it was scarcely conceivable that the Americans would choose to dump their war leader when within sight of victory.

Roosevelt died in April, 1945, shortly after returning from the Yalta peace conference, where, with Winston Churchill and Josef Stalin, he created a blueprint for post-war Europe. His successor was Harry Truman, the former senator from Missouri whose selection as vice-presidential candidate at the Democratic convention had been the subject of more controversy than Roosevelt's re-nomination as President. Roosevelt's twelve years in office make him by far the longest-serving President. Although they were successful years, Congress was worried by the precedent and moved swiftly to ensure that nobody should serve as long again. The Twenty-second Amendment to the Constitution, proposed in 1947 and ratified in 1951, limits Presidents to two terms, unless they have succeeded to the office with less than two years of a term to run, in which case they may contest two elections. For most, eight years is long enough.

That amendment is characteristic of the way the institution of the presidency has been adapted, almost by trial and error, throughout its history. Confronted for the first time with a President elected to four terms, Congress decided that this was not the way the institution should run; so it was modified. Ever since the coming of party politics provoked the first major change in the concept of the office, its powers and duties have been altered over the years in response to the personality of the incumbent and the desires of Congress.

Truman's tenure illustrated another salient point about the modern presidency. He was the chirpy, unexceptional son of a modest mid-western farmer. He worked for ten years on his father's farm, then became a haberdasher, until the business failed. That was when he went into politics. It has long been an article of faith among Americans that any citizen can aspire to the highest office in the land. Truman was proof of that.

2

Post-War Presidents

Harry S. Truman, 1945–53

Vice-presidential candidates have not generally been chosen because they are suitable to take over the top job. Although several Presidents have died in office – and one resigned – the optimistic nature of any political campaign means that a full term is normally anticipated. The priority is to balance the ticket: a northerner will run with a southerner, a liberal with a conservative, to broaden their appeal.

The choice of Harry Truman as vice-presidential candidate to Franklin Roosevelt was an exception to this rule. Roosevelt had suffered from polio as a child and was usually in a wheelchair. By 1944, he had borne bravely the strain of twelve years in office, three of them in wartime. Although he was in reasonable health during the campaign, and was only sixty-two years old, it was in the back of everyone's mind that he might not survive a fourth term. In Truman, therefore, the Democrats consciously chose a man who shared Roosevelt's philosophy and had the capacity to fill his shoes in the event of his premature departure. That happened sooner than anyone expected, in April 1945, less than six months after the election. Truman was immediately sworn in as President. The war in Europe ended the following month and he began a round of international conferences as the world began to pull itself together after the turmoil.

Within months he was faced with one of the most momentous decisions a world leader has ever had to make. The war in the Pacific appeared to be won but the Japanese would not surrender and there was the prospect of more prolonged fighting and loss of life. The Americans now had in their possession the atomic bomb, with the power to cause massive devastation, as well as long-term effects that would not be fully understood for many years.

Only the President could decide whether to open this new deadly chapter in modern warfare, or whether to let the conflict drag on. There have been few occasions when the awesome responsibilities of the office have been illustrated so dramatically. On 6 August Truman authorised an atomic bomb attack on the Japanese port of Hiroshima and three days later on Nagasaki, virtually destroying both cities and causing nearly a million casualties. Whether the decision was correct is a question that will never, by its nature, be resolved to everyone's satisfaction: but it had the desired effect, for the following week Japan surrendered.

At the time, in the heat of war, Truman's action received overwhelming support from Americans. They badly wanted to find in him a man they could unite behind to pursue in peacetime the policies of his predecessor. Inevitably, though, the glow of affection in which he was held during his first hectic months of office was destined to dim when America faced post-war realities. Servicemen, like those from other Allied nations, returned from the battlefields with a heightened sense of their worth. This showed itself in a series of strikes as the trade unions sought to assert their rights. When strikes occurred in key industries such as the railways, steel and coal, Truman temporarily put them under government control to ensure continuity of production – actions that alienated the owners, who would have preferred to settle their labour problems by attrition.

Truman met more resistance when he tried to extend the welfare provisions of the New Deal. Although when he took office the Democrats had a majority in both houses, there was a right-wing faction, mainly from the southern states, that often voted with the Republicans on social issues. This coalition of the right succeeded in blocking or weakening measures to control prices, improve public housing and bar racial discrimination in employment. In the 1946 mid-term elections, the Republicans won control of both houses, putting the legislature in direct conflict with the executive. Congress overrode Truman's vetoes on measures such as the Taft-Hartley Act, restricting the power of the trade unions. The embittered President characterised the eightieth Congress as the worst in history.

In international affairs, Truman's policies continued to receive bi-partisan support, largely because world war was quickly followed by cold war and the nation could unite against the perceived threat from the East. There was little controversy about the Marshall Plan, by which the United States undertook to assist Europe in its post-war reconstruction. Apart from the humanitarian arguments, this was seen as a means of strengthening the Western world against possible incursion and subversion by the communists, a strategy that came to be known as the Truman Doctrine and one on which American foreign policy was based for decades. The creation of the North Atlantic Treaty Organisation (NATO) in 1949 sprang from the same philosophy.

Nor, this time, was there any serious doubt that the United States would play its full part in the United Nations, the world body that was to replace the League of Nations. The war, with its ghastly demonstration of what happens when international order breaks down, seemed finally to have cured the majority of Americans of their isolationist predilections. To symbolise the American commitment it was agreed that the headquarters of the UN should be in New York. The US also took the lead in establishing a World Bank and International Monetary Fund. Truman favoured these initiatives and was able to steer them through Congress with little difficulty, even though there was still an isolationist rump in the two houses, chiefly on the Republican side.

But because of the opposition of Congress to his domestic policies, Truman seemed to have no chance of re-election in 1948. The north-south split in his party had resulted in the southern Democrats – the Dixiecrats – putting up a rival candidate in Strom Thurmond, Governor of South Carolina. And Henry Wallace of the Progressive Party threatened to siphon off the votes of some left-wing Democrats.

Truman would not admit defeat. He travelled more than 30,000 miles on a nationwide tour, making speeches attacking Congress. He was one of the few people in Washington who believed his victory was possible. Opinion polls and political commentators put his opponent, Thomas Dewey, well in the lead. One newspaper even printed an edition announcing Dewey's victory. Despite these doubts, however, Truman came through by a comfortable majority in the electoral college, if more narrowly in the popular vote.

The cold war dominated his second term. In 1949 a communist government took control in China. Some Americans believed that Truman could and should have done more to bolster the ousted leader Chiang Kai-Shek. The United States continued to recognise Chiang's regime in Formosa (Taiwan) as the legitimate government of China but this did not appease those who urged greater US involvement in defending non-communist regimes in Asia. Anger over the 'loss' of China was an important part of the reason for getting involved in the war in Korea.

That small Far Eastern country had been divided after World War Two into a northern part, controlled by communists, and a southern area allied to the United States. In June 1950 troops from the north invaded the south. The United Nations Security Council, with the Russians absent because of a boycott, agreed to establish a force to counter the aggression from the north. American troops dominated the force and it was under the command of US General Douglas MacArthur, hero of the war in the Pacific. The communist Chinese entered the war on the side of North Korea and hostilities lasted for three years, with two million people killed, including 54,000 Americans. Truman was forced to dismiss MacArthur, who had wanted to carry the war to China.

Internally, the Korean war fuelled a deep hostility to communism, allied with the suspicion that many secret communist sympathisers worked in the US government – especially the State Department – and in other areas of

American life, such as the film industry. Senator Joseph McCarthy, a Republican demagogue from Wisconsin, was chairman of a congressional committee that held a series of hearings where suspected communists were denounced in the atmosphere of a witch-hunt. Many were forced to leave their jobs. In the film industry a notorious 'black list' was drawn up of people not to be hired by the major Hollywood studios. To begin with, McCarthy and his committee enjoyed considerable popular support.

Truman could have run for a third term in 1952. The constitutional amendment ratified in 1951, limiting Presidents to two terms, specifically excluded the President in office at the time of ratification. But early in 1952 he announced that he would not be a candidate. With a show of reluctance, Governor Adlai Stevenson of Illinois was made the Democratic nominee, but the Republicans trumped him by persuading General Dwight Eisenhower, hero of the war in Europe, to stand for them. Affectionately nicknamed 'Ike', he was one of the country's best-known and best-liked personalities.

The Eisenhower camp exploited the anti-communist mood by choosing as their vice-presidential candidate Senator Richard Nixon of California, who as a congressman had been active on the House Un-American Activities Committee. When the Democrats sought to smear Nixon by revealing that he was backed financially by a group of Californian millionaires, he saved the day with an impassioned half-hour television appearance. It has become known as the Checkers speech (see page 91) and, as the first time that television had played a decisive role in the nation's politics, had a profound influence on the future style of presidential campaigning.

The Eisenhower/Nixon ticket won convincingly. With the Korean war still being fought, it was not surprising that the voters should return to the tradition of a soldier in the White House. The Republicans had regained the presidency after twenty years.

Dwight D. Eisenhower, 1953–1961

Eisenhower represented the liberal wing of the Republican party and had won the nomination after a hard fight against the conservative Senator Robert Taft. With his experience in Europe (his last job as a soldier had been commander-in-chief of NATO forces) he was almost inevitably an internationalist. There was now no possibility of the United States retreating to its post-World War One isolationism: foreign affairs became an increasing preoccupation with Eisenhower and his successors. The Secretary of State, John Foster Dulles, became the most influential of his Cabinet colleagues.

The new President's first priority was to end the war in Korea. In June 1953, five months after his inauguration, a peace treaty was signed, leaving Korea divided at the thirty-eighth parallel as before.

Another Far Eastern war was under way that did not then involve the United States directly but which was to exert a profound influence on its future. The French were being forced from their protectorates in Indo-China – Vietnam, Laos and Cambodia. In the spring of 1954 the Vietnamese communists under Ho Chi Minh inflicted the final defeat on the French at Dien Bien Phu. At the subsequent Geneva conference, Vietnam was divided into the communist north and non-communist south, with a commitment to reunify the country after elections in 1956.

The elections did not take place. Meanwhile Eisenhower had written to the South Vietnamese President, Ngo Dinh Diem, offering aid 'to assist the government of Vietnam in developing a strong, viable state, capable of resisting attempted subversion or aggression through military means'. In return, President Diem would be expected to introduce governmental reforms. From that letter flowed the costly and damaging US entanglement in Vietnam that would not be unravelled for nearly twenty years.

Domestically, Eisenhower's views on welfare and public expenditure were so liberal that he found it easier to work with the Democrat-controlled Congress, elected in 1954, than

when Republicans were in a majority. He was heartily
opposed to Senator McCarthy's witch-hunts against alleged
communist sympathisers, but was criticised by some liberals
for not making his views plainer in public. In the event
McCarthy was censured by the Senate, forfeited his chairmanship of the Committee for Un-American Activities and
had lost his influence by the time he died in 1957. But his short
spell in the limelight caused grave and long-lasting damage to
the tolerant image of themselves that Americans sought to
foster.

Eisenhower persuaded Congress to sustain a generous
foreign aid programme and in 1955 underlined his inter-
nationalism by attending a summit meeting with Soviet,
British and French leaders in Geneva. Soon afterwards he
suffered a mild heart attack but this did not stop him from
running for office again in 1956. Such was his popularity,
coupled with the nation's rising prosperity, that there was
never any real doubt that he would defeat Adlai Stevenson
again, this time by an even greater margin than before.

In the last two weeks of the campaign two major foreign
issues blew up. The first was the despatch of Soviet tanks to
Hungary to suppress moves towards liberalising the communist regime. Almost simultaneously the British and French
launched an ill-judged military intervention in Egypt to try
to wrest back the Suez Canal after its nationalisation by
President Nasser. Eisenhower and Dulles believed that both
invasions conflicted with the anti-colonialist mood that pre-
vailed in the post-war world, and flouted the United Nations
charter. Even had they wanted to stand aloof from the Suez
conflict, that would have been inconsistent with their vigorous
condemnation of the Russians in Hungary. The United States
initiated UN resolutions calling for a Middle East ceasefire.
Within days, the lack of American support forced the British
and French to withdraw. As far as the election was concerned,
the two foreign crises probably helped Eisenhower in that
they persuaded the electorate of the need to vote back into
office an experienced statesman at a time of external threats.

His second term began with a domestic issue of extreme

difficulty and sensitivity. In 1954 the Supreme Court, in the case of Brown *v*. the Board of Education, had ruled against racial segregation in American schools. The ruling was bitterly opposed in much of the south and in 1957 Orval Faubus, the governor of Arkansas, defied it by refusing to countenance integration in the state. Eisenhower sent federal troops to Little Rock, the state capital, to enforce the court's decision. He knew that the action would arouse great passion in the south and could even rekindle the embers of the Civil War, but he had no doubt that his first responsibility as President was to uphold the law. That was why he was obliged to accept the resignation of his administrative assistant, Sherman Adams, in the worst scandal of his two terms. Adams fell from grace when his name was linked with that of Bernard Goldfine, a businessman under investigation by a congressional committee. Adams had received gifts from Goldfine including a vicuna coat.

In the same year, American troops were on the move again, this time overseas to the Lebanon. Since Suez, nationalism in the Middle East had prospered and a number of pro-Western or neutral regimes had been replaced by leaders backed, either overtly or covertly, by the Soviet Union. When that happened in Iraq, Lebanon's President Chamoun feared that his own government was at risk and asked for US military assistance. Eisenhower responded by despatching 9,000 marines and a fleet of seventy ships. It was ironic that the United States should be sending a force to the Middle East less than two years after opposing the British and French action at Suez, but Eisenhower defended the decision by pointing out that it was done at the request of a friendly sovereign government. After four months the force was replaced by a contingent under the control of the United Nations.

For some years after he left office, the popular image of Eisenhower's presidency was of complacency and inaction. He was often photographed on the golf course, which allowed easy jokes about not giving his full attention to affairs of state. There were two reasons for this – personal and political. He

was by nature not a flamboyant man and he was consti-
tutionally opposed to the all-powerful imperial presidency: he
sought to keep himself strictly to the duties of the office, not to
expand them. The political reason was that he had to live with
a Democrat-dominated Congress, which, despite his liberalism, increasingly limited his scope for initiating legislation
with a hope of success.

He was, however, held in immense popular affection
throughout his term of office, for his affability and ease of
manner. He was the first President to allow televised press
conferences and he took lessons in self-projection from the
actor Robert Montgomery. In the end, he may have been too
much the patrician to suit the mood of a country about to
enter the turbulence of the 1960s. But as time goes on, his
performance as President is being reassessed. In a period of
fast social and economic change, he provided the nation with
the stability it craved.

John F. Kennedy, 1961–2

The divided views about the Eisenhower era were reflected in
the 1960 election, which ended virtually in a dead-heat in
terms of the popular vote. Richard Nixon, the former Vice-
President, won 34,106,671 votes and John Kennedy, his
Democratic opponent, 34,221,344. The result in the electoral
college hinged on some disputed returns from Illinois and
Texas. They went Kennedy's way and the former senator
from Massachusetts became the country's first Roman Catholic President. In his inaugural speech he said: 'Let the word
go forth from this time and place, to friend and foe alike, that
the torch has been passed to a new generation of Americans.'

The new President was the eldest surviving son of Joseph
Kennedy, who had been the United States ambassador to
Britain at the start of World War Two – unpopular in the host
country because of his opposition to US entry into the war.
(His eldest son was killed in the fighting later.) The Kennedys
were a large but cohesive Boston political family with Irish

antecedents. His campaign for the presidency had been under way almost since 1956, when he came surprisingly close to winning the Democratic nomination for Vice-President. It was bankrolled by his wealthy family – as his Senate campaigns had been – and his relatives played prominent roles in its organisation. He had no compunction about appointing his brother Robert as his attorney-general, or his brother-in-law Sargent Shriver to head the Peace Corps, a new and idealistic organisation that sent Americans to lend expertise and technical help to developing countries.

Kennedy's election was interpreted as a reaction against the soporific, autumnal quality of the last years of Eisenhower. There were to be no more afternoons on the golf course, no more letting things ride. The new President, a war hero, was only forty-three years old – twenty-seven years younger than his predecessor. He was energetic and interventionist. Instructions and messages and executive orders flowed from the Oval Office. He attracted some of the most gifted academics to work for him in Washington, a city that had previously shown more respect for the exercise of power than for matters of the mind.

His patronage of the arts was also something rare in modern chief executives. He and his vivacious wife Jackie went to concerts, plays and art galleries. They almost immediately began introducing contemporary art and furnishings into the White House. They and their two young children caught the nation's imagination. Jackie became more of a celebrity than any First Lady before or since: the press wrote about her endlessly, meticulously documenting what she did and said, what she wore and where she went. They were a physical family. They swam, they did workouts, they played tennis and touch football. They attracted to Washington a community of clever and lively young people in their own image. The press dubbed it Camelot, after the legendary court and capital of King Arthur and his knights.

But the administration's initial air of confidence and success was quickly shattered by reality, and in particular by a botched and misguided attempt by the Central Intelligence Agency, with Kennedy's approval, to launch a rebellion against Fidel Castro's communist regime in Cuba. Anti-communist exiles based in Guatemala had been formed into a force that planned to land at the Bay of Pigs, march on Havana and seize power. The landing was poorly organised and repelled with ease. It was a disastrous, ill-judged beginning for a presidency in which liberal Americans had vested such hope.

Its effect on Kennedy's international reputation was its gravest long-term consequence. It convinced Nikita Khrushchev, the fiery leader of the Soviet Union, that Kennedy was a weak and inexperienced President, surrounded by incompetent advisers. The two men met at a summit conference in Vienna in June 1961 – one of the most disastrous meetings ever held between an American and a Russian leader. The Russians were anxious to 'solve' the question of Berlin, by which they meant ending the four-power occupation of the former German capital and incorporating it into communist East Germany. The meeting was rancorous and served only to increase international tension. Returning from it, both leaders took steps to strengthen their countries' defence forces. In August the East Germans built the Berlin wall to prevent their citizens from defecting to the West. It was to remain a permanent symbol of the cold war.

In other parts of the world, Kennedy felt it necessary to take a tough line, if only to convince Khrushchev of his weight as an opponent. He sent more 'advisers' to Vietnam to strengthen the 685 already there, and he gave more military aid to the Saigon regime, although he resisted calls to send combat troops. His severest test came in October 1962, when aerial reconnaissance of Cuba showed that the Russians had built sites there for inter-continental ballistic missiles that could reach the United States three minutes after being launched. Kennedy demanded that the missiles be withdrawn and announced a blockade of Cuba. Ships carrying missiles or components to the island would be intercepted. A fleet of twenty-five merchant ships, presumed to be carrying such material, was steaming towards Cuba. World war looked closer than at any time for fifteen years.

The ships carrying missiles did not, in the event, brave the American blockade. On 28 October, after a nail-biting week of crisis, Khrushchev announced that the missiles would be dismantled. Kennedy lifted the blockade and the world was safe again, at least comparatively. It was a considerable triumph for the young President and enormously increased his international stature.

At home, the Kennedy term was dominated by racial tension, as blacks sought to assert rights of equality that powerful members of the white community would not voluntarily cede. In the first months of his term the 'freedom riders' took a bus through southern states to challenge segregation in public places. There were a number of confrontations with local whites but serious violence was avoided, if narrowly.

The following year saw a long legal battle by James Meredith, a black man, to register at the all-white University of Mississippi. The state governor led the opposition to his enrolment, which was only finally achieved after intervention by troops of the National Guard. Eighteen months later there was a similar confrontation at the University of Alabama, where the state governor, George Wallace, tried to prevent two black students from enrolling. Earlier in the year Wallace had clashed with the most prominent black civil rights leader, Martin Luther King, who was campaigning for an end to segregation in the state. In August King led a march on Washington, where he made his renowned 'I have a dream' speech: 'I have a dream that one day this nation will rise up, live out the true meaning of its creed.'

Kennedy was keen to sponsor legislation on civil rights – as on other social issues – but he had difficulty in handling Congress, most of whose members did not readily identify with the thrusting young people surrounding the President. His proposals on free health care for the elderly, better social security and rebuilding inner cities became bogged down in the legislative process. He had better luck with his initiative on space exploration. Mortified by Soviet successes in space, he vowed that the United States would put a man on the moon by the end of the decade.

Despite his difficulties with Congress, Kennedy and his family remained popular and there seemed little doubt, in November 1963, that he would be re-elected in a year's time. Then on 22 November 1963, on a visit to Texas as an early part of the next year's campaign, he was shot dead while being driven through the streets of Dallas. The suspect, Lee Harvey Oswald, was himself shot dead by Jack Ruby two days later. Because of Oswald's death, some questions arising from the assassination have never been solved in a wholly satisfactory manner. Numerous conspiracy theories have been concocted, for like all powerful leaders Kennedy had a wide selection of enemies. But the simplest explanation remains the most likely: Oswald was operating alone.

The nation's reaction to the assassination of its President was one of stunned horror, outrage and an irredeemable sense of loss. This was especially so among young people, who had identified with Kennedy more than with any other President in history. Questions were asked about the kind of society that could foster an act of such barbarism. The anger and bitterness engendered by the tragedy had much to do with the sour, disillusioned mood of the nation's youth that was a feature of the late 1960s.

The cruel curtailment of his term makes it hard to assess Kennedy's performance in the White House. Had he lived, he might have become a great President. He could not yet be counted as such by the time he died.

Lyndon B. Johnson, 1963–1969

With a President nine years younger than him, Vice-President Lyndon Johnson had not expected to succeed to the office. The tall, loose-limbed Texan, with a fondness for cowboy hats, had been Kennedy's chief opponent for the Democratic nomination in 1960. Kennedy had put him on the ticket primarily because he balanced it regionally. Moreover his crude, studiedly uncultured approach to life counteracted the sophistication of the Kennedys and appealed to that important section of the community, strongest in the south and mid-west, who regarded the Kennedy style as effete.

Johnson was no part of Camelot. He had little time for most of the young, brainy advisers who had surrounded Kennedy. The lack of sympathy was mutual: Kennedy's people could not forgive Johnson for not being Kennedy. In the aftermath of the assassination, the new President made no immediate changes in the Cabinet and few to the White House staff. But even before the 1964 election, the Kennedy people began to drift away.

Johnson had been a congressman from 1937, when he was twenty-nine and an enthusiastic supporter of Roosevelt's New Deal. He was elected to the Senate in 1948 and from 1955 led the Democratic majority there. His skill was in cajoling politicians to his way of thinking, in manufacturing majorities in initially unpromising circumstances. Arm-squeezing and back-slapping were the tools of his trade.

They came into their own in the situation he inherited from Kennedy. The social reform measures that had been blocked by Congress were given a new lease of life, by dint both of Johnson's persuasive techniques and because of the feeling in Washington that the murdered President needed a tangible memorial. An anti-poverty measure was enacted, with an appropriation of £784 million for its first year. Kennedy's plan for free medical treatment for the elderly (Medicare) went into law, as did his Civil Rights Act, strengthened by a Voting Rights Act the following year. A more permissive immigration law was passed and a Cabinet office established for urban affairs. Federal aid for education was increased. In the 1964 election campaign, Johnson coined a phrase for his social reforms: the Great Society.

It was ironic that these legislative measures should coincide with the first of what came to be known as the 'long, hot summers' of the mid-1960s, which saw violent disturbances in many black-populated inner city areas. It started in Harlem, the black section of New York City, which endured three

nights of rioting and looting in July 1964. The trouble spread
to Brooklyn, Chicago, Philadelphia and several smaller cities
in New Jersey and New York. The following year the worst
riots of all occurred in Watts, a suburb of Los Angeles, where
in six days of disturbances thirty-four people were killed and
900 injured. Militant black power movements sprang up, the
most prominent the Black Muslims and the Black Panthers.

Overseas, too, there were fresh signs of trouble to come.
Things had been getting worse in Vietnam throughout 1963
and 1964: corruption and mismanagement in Saigon meant
that much of America's aid was squandered. The North
Vietnamese were making gains in spite of the growing number of United States advisers in the south. In August 1964 the
North Vietnamese fired on an American destroyer in the Gulf
of Tonkin in what Johnson called 'open aggression on the high
seas'. (Reports some years later cast doubt on who was the
aggressor.) Johnson sought and received from Congress the
authority to take 'necessary measures' to combat further
attacks on US forces, and to 'prevent further aggression'. This
measure, known as the Tonkin Gulf Resolution, gave the
President unchecked powers to escalate the Vietnam war and
to commit American combat troops to it.

In political terms Johnson's initiative was popular and
timely, for in November he was to seek re-election against an
opponent from the right wing of the Republican Party, Senator Barry Goldwater. One of the themes of Goldwater's
campaign was the need to take a tough line against communism. He advocated the dispatch of American troops and
aircraft to finish the war quickly. Johnson, by his action, had
cut much of the ground from under his opponent's feet. But
during the campaign he insisted that he was against 'American boys' doing the fighting for Asians. The 190 American
advisers already killed there were more than enough.

Goldwater was much too extreme in his views for a nation
that only four years earlier had elected the liberal John
Kennedy to the White House. Johnson won an enormous
victory by 486 electoral college votes to fifty-two. At the
beginning of 1965 the Viet Cong, the communist guerillas in

Vietnam, launched a series of attacks on targets where American advisers were stationed. Many American lives were lost and Johnson accepted the advice of the 'hawks' among his entourage. Using the authority given him by the Tonkin Gulf Resolution, he authorised heavy American bombing raids into North Vietnam. In the first three months of the year the number of American servicemen in Vietnam was tripled from 25,000 to 75,000 and in April a further 40,000 were dispatched. In June the President authorised the use of American troops in combat to support the South Vietnamese when needed. In July another 50,000 troops were committed and the number of young men drafted into the services was doubled. America had entered a war almost without noticing it.

That year saw the beginning of the protests against the war, started by students, that were to be a feature of American life until the troops were withdrawn eight years later. Some men who had been picked for the draft publicly burned their draft cards. Others fled to Canada or Europe to avoid conscription. In time the demonstrations spread from university campuses and gained the support of the middle-aged and the middle class, although there were counter-protests from conservatives who supported the war. With more civil rights disturbances in the south, and more inner city rioting, the great issues of American life were coming to be fought on the streets.

The protests did not deter Johnson. More and more troops were committed to the war. By April 1967 the total was 480,000, a year later 549,000. By then nearly 23,000 Americans had been killed in the war. But even that level of commitment could not prevent a major communist victory during the Tet offensive of 1968, when several key South Vietnamese cities were lost. General Westmoreland, the commander of the US force, asked for 200,000 more men.

It was a presidential election year and opposition to Johnson's war policy was increasing. More and more people were alarmed by the extent of the American commitment, the mounting casualties and – the most potent influence of all –

the horrifying pictures from the front that appeared on the
television news every night. Opposition to communism, and
fears of its taking root in the United States, had bred support
for US involvement, but the price was now seen to be
unacceptably high. Isolationism, never far below the surface
of American thinking, began to seem an attractive option.

In the New Hampshire primary in March Eugene
McCarthy, a senator running on the policy of US withdrawal
from the war, won forty-two per cent of the Democratic vote,
against Johnson's forty-eight per cent. This close result had a
shattering effect on Johnson. At the end of the month he went
on television to announce that he did not want to involve the
presidency in the bitter political divisions in the country. He
would therefore not seek or accept nomination for another
term. The Democratic nomination soon became a three-way
contest between Vice-President Hubert Humphrey, John
Kennedy's brother, Robert, and the peace campaigner
Eugene McCarthy.

All years have their high and low points but 1968 was one of
the most traumatic in United States history. In April Martin
Luther King, the country's most prominent black civil rights
leader, was shot dead on the balcony of a motel in Memphis,
Tennessee. Two months later in Los Angeles Robert
Kennedy, celebrating a victory in the California primary that
would probably have won him the Democratic nomination,
was shot and killed at the Ambassador Hotel. The Democratic convention was held in Chicago against a background of
violent clashes between peace demonstrators and police in
what investigators later called a 'police riot'.

None of that helped the chance of Vice-President
Humphrey, the Democratic nominee. Johnson's failure to
extricate himself from the Vietnam quagmire further
lengthened the odds against a Democratic victory. The
Republican candidate was the durable Richard Nixon, who
promised to end American involvement in the war. Nixon had
the advantage of being associated with what in retrospect
were seen as the safe, certain days of Eisenhower. The
Americans had elected John Kennedy in 1960 because he

promised excitement. Now they felt they had experienced rather too much of that.

During the campaign Nixon cast his running mate Spiro Agnew, former Governor of Maryland, in the role of the scourge of the radicals. They were elected, but only narrowly in terms of the popular vote: less than one per cent. Governor George Wallace of Alabama, an opponent of integration, put up the best performance by a third party candidate for years, winning nearly ten million votes, or 13.5 per cent.

So for Nixon, at least, the dreadful year of 1968 ended on a high note. And there was another straw to clutch at. Apart from the disturbances at the Democratic convention in Chicago, American cities had their most peaceful summer for four years. A calmer mood was beginning to prevail as Johnson left the White House after a presidency that had begun and ended in tragedy and, dragged down by the appalling misjudgments in Vietnam, was never able to fulfil his hopes.

Richard M. Nixon, 1969–74

A few months after Nixon began his term, a much-needed fillip was provided for American morale when two astronauts, watched by the world on live television, set foot on the moon, fulfilling President Kennedy's timetable of getting there before the end of the decade. Yet while it gave the new presidency an optimistic start, it did not silence the still vociferous critics of the Vietnam involvement. Although Nixon had promised during the campaign to pull American troops out, to do so peremptorily would lead to a rapid communist takeover and an unacceptable loss of prestige. He decided on a policy of 'Vietnamisation', meaning the replacement of all American troops by Vietnamese. That had been the original strategy behind the commitment of American advisers eight years earlier. It had not been found practical then and many doubted whether it was feasible at this stage.

Announcing the plan, Nixon asked for the support 'of the

great silent majority of my fellow Americans', meaning those who did not take part in – indeed deplored – the anti-war protests. This signalled the beginning of a strategy of counter-attack against liberal and radical critics of his administration, spearheaded by his Vice-President, Spiro Agnew, whose speechwriters invented some vivid phrases for him. The President's critics, he said, were 'an effete corps of impudent snobs who characterise themselves as intellectuals'. He weighed into liberal journalists in the press and television as an 'unelected elite'. The conviction that they spoke for the majority of real Americans, whose way of life was threatened by loose liberal values, provided the justification, in the minds of the Nixon administration, for the excesses that finally led to disaster.

In the early days opinion polls indicated support for this populist position. But the unsilent minority refused to be silenced, and 1968 saw an escalation of anti-war protests on college campuses. Feelings were heightened with the revelation of a massacre of South Vietnamese civilians by American troops at the hamlet of My Lai.

The war did not abate and Nixon seemed at a loss as to how to carry out his commitment to withdraw American troops. In May 1970, indeed, he extended it by authorising US infantry to move into Cambodia, which provided sanctuary for Viet Cong soldiers. The Americans had already been secretly bombing Cambodia for a year. Campus protests increased. At Kent State in Ohio, four students were killed and nine wounded when national guardsmen fired on demonstrators. Tens of thousands of students marched on Washington. Nixon, in a curious gesture, slipped out of the White House with his security men in the middle of the night in an unfruitful attempt to engage some protestors in dialogue. Despite aggressive campaigning by the President and Vice-President, the Republicans lost ground in the 1970 mid-term elections.

The Vietnam war was beginning to have the same effect on Nixon as it had had on Johnson. Against his will, it was dominating his presidency. He felt trapped and impotent. His reaction was to turn on his enemies and tighten his own defences. He set up security and intelligence systems in the White House far more extensive than any of his predecessors. A series of embarrassing press revelations fed his paranoia, culminating in the publication in the *New York Times* of the Pentagon Papers, a secret government study into the origins of the Vietnam involvement. Nixon ordered telephone taps on some journalists and officials to try to stem such leaks. At the same time plots were hatched against political opponents, including possible adversaries in the 1972 election. Nixon and his aides believed that only an all-powerful presidency – an 'imperial presidency', as it came to be called – could protect the nation's soul from the perils that assailed it.

The weakness of the Vietnamisation policy became apparent at the beginning of 1971 when 16,000 Vietnamese troops tried to cut the Viet Cong supply route – the Ho Chi Minh trail – in Laos. Nearly a quarter of them were killed and more than 5,000 wounded. Nixon and his foreign affairs adviser Henry Kissinger could see no way of withdrawing American troops before the election.

By good timing, though, they were able to capitalise on a foreign policy triumph that caught the public's imagination. In the summer of 1971, following overtures from the Chinese communists and an exchange of visits by the two countries' table tennis teams, Kissinger went to Peking and arranged for Nixon to pay an official visit to China the following February, to meet the legendary party chairman, Mao Tse-tung, and the Prime Minister, Chou En-lai. It was an extraordinary piece of gymnastics from a President who had effectively built his career on rigid anti-communism when he sat on the Committee for Un-American Activities in the 1950s. He had to sacrifice his former unequivocal support for the Chinese Nationalists in Taiwan, but it was a small price to pay for such a spectacular diplomatic triumph.

Three months later Nixon went East again, this time to Moscow for talks with the Communist Party Chairman, Leonid Brezhnev. The Russians were nervous about the rapprochement between the US and China – the two powers they looked on with most suspicion. Nixon was made welcome in Moscow and several agreements were signed on collaborative projects and arms limitation. The political benefits of the two visits in an election year were immeasurable. And by the autumn Kissinger had begun exploratory peace talks with the North Vietnamese in Paris.

Nixon was assured of the Republican nomination. For the Democrats, Senator Edmund Muskie was the early frontrunner, but he faded. A contest developed between Governor George Wallace, Hubert Humphrey and Senator George McGovern. Wallace became another victim of an attempted assassination when he was shot at Laurel, Maryland, and paralysed from the waist down. McGovern, the peace candidate, won the nomination but what slender chance he had of victory was destroyed by the way he handled the revelation that his choice as running mate, Senator Thomas Eagleton, had a history of mental instability.

The capture of five burglars at the offices of the Democratic National Committee in Washington's Watergate building on 17 June 1972 was not widely reported. They were trying to bug telephones on behalf of the Republicans but there was no evidence then that the White House was involved, despite the efforts of two reporters on the *Washington Post* to discover just where the responsibility should be pinned. Nixon won the election with majorities in every state except Massachusetts and the District of Columbia.

Soon after the election the Vietnam peace talks, which until then had looked promising, broke down, partly because of objections from the South Vietnamese. Nixon authorised massive bombing raids over the north. These caused thousands of casualties but many aircraft were also lost. Both sides had the incentive to resume talks, and the Paris meetings began again in January. At the end of the month a treaty was signed. American troops were withdrawn. The war had cost 57,000 American lives and more than 100,000 serious injuries. Without the Americans, South Vietnam did not last long. In May 1975 the communists entered Saigon and united Vietnam under their rule.

But Nixon was by then not in the White House to denounce

the perfidy of the North Vietnamese. Throughout 1973 and for part of 1974, he was weighed down by the Watergate affair. Each revelation served to suggest his complicity in the attempt to cover up White House involvement in the burglary. There were Congressional hearings. The Special Prosecutor appointed to investigate the affair indicted several men who were formerly Nixon's closest colleagues. To compound his embarrassment, in October 1973 Vice-President Agnew was forced to resign after allegations that as Governor of Maryland he had accepted bribes from architects and builders in return for the award of contracts.

Until 1967 there had been no provision for the replacement of a Vice-President, or for the appointment of a new one should the Vice-President succeed to the presidency. The Twenty-fifth Amendment to the Constitution, ratified that year, allowed the President to pick a new Vice-President, subject to the approval of Congress. Nixon chose Gerald Ford, the Republican leader in the House of Representatives, described by the commentator Alistair Cooke as 'a reliable party hack of amiable small stature'.

In the summer of 1974, two years after the break-in, Nixon was finally forced to release the tape recording of a conversation that proved he had initiated the Watergate cover-up a few days after the burglary and had since lied about his involvement. He would certainly have been impeached by Congress had he not resigned on 8 August 1974 – the first American President to do so.

Gerald R. Ford, 1974–7

After a month in office President Ford performed the most controversial act of his presidency and the one that may have cost him a second term. He decided to give President Nixon a blanket pardon for any offences he might have committed over Watergate. There were sound reasons for the decision. A trial of the former President would certainly have exacerbated the national wounds that Ford was trying to heal. The country had already been absorbed for the best part of two years with the Watergate affair and it was time for a change in the agenda.

All the same, the pardon was unpopular. Many of Nixon's subordinates had been convicted of Watergate-related offences and were serving jail sentences. Why should the ringleader go free? And Ford had not agreed an unconditional total amnesty for Vietnam draft evaders: they would have to carry out two years' community service to purge their offence. His critics pointed out that many draft-dodgers had, after all, acted for conscientious reasons. Nixon's motive had simply been to hold on to his power. There were suspicions – vigorously denied – that Nixon had only agreed to go, or effectively to hand power to Ford, on condition that he was promised a full pardon. An unsuccessful attempt was made to challenge the move in the courts, on the grounds that you cannot pardon a man who has not been indicted or convicted.

Ford's was very much an interim presidency. While Alistair Cooke's verdict on him may have been harsh, few could think of a more flattering word than 'amiable' to describe him. He was thought to be intellectually limited, more interested in football – which he played well in his youth – than in matters of the mind. He had a reputation for clumsiness, both physical and mental. If he stumbled climbing down from an aircraft, or fell over while skiing, or bumped his head, a camera was always there to record the event. His spontaneous answers to press questions were often less than agile. Scurrilous jokes went the rounds about his difficulty in walking in a straight line and chewing gum at the same time. When he made some controversial Cabinet changes in 1975, the columnist Joseph Kraft wrote of 'new doubts as to whether he has the brains to be President'.

Ford's healing mission was effective in terms of the Watergate trauma, which did in time become less acute; but other wounds opened up. Tension in the Middle East grew worse and neither he nor Kissinger, shuttling between the capitals, could bring the Arabs and the Israelis together. The war pushed up the price of oil, and the resulting energy crisis aggravated the severe recession. He had to preside over the humiliating evacuation of the last Americans from Saigon, without the power to prevent it. (Even had he wanted to send troops to bolster the South Vietnamese, it was harder to do that since the passage by Congress in 1973 of the War Powers Resolution, which limited the President's power to deploy troops abroad without congressional authority.) Congress also prevented him from sending aid to the pro-Western regime in Angola to help fight communist rebels.

In two summit meetings with Leonid Brezhnev, no progress was made on further arms limitation measures. The 1975 Helsinki conference on security and co-operation in Europe produced impressive communiqués which did not amount to much in practice. Similarly, Ford's visit to China in November of that year inspired plenty of press coverage but few concrete results.

The most visible effects of the recession were on the nation's inner cities – and because New York was the biggest of them, it suffered more than the others. It was going through one of its recurrent periods of near-bankruptcy and was lobbying hard for federal aid. Ford took a rigorous conservative line against too much help from the centre for the inner cities – a line popular with non-urban Middle America, the source of much Republican support, but naturally resented in the cities themselves. The New York view was summed up in this memorable front page headline in the *Daily News*: FORD TO CITY: DROP DEAD.

In his campaign for election for a full term in 1976, Ford first had to overcome a strong challenge from inside his own party. It is rare for an incumbent President to meet any serious competition for his party's nomination, but Ford was more vulnerable than most because he had not originally been chosen by the party as their candidate, but had been appointed to the vice-presidency by the disgraced Nixon. In electoral terms, his association with Nixon – highlighted by the granting of a pardon – could be a liability. And the recession had given new impetus to the low-tax, low-spending theories of the Republican right, for whom Ford was too much of a centrist.

The candidate of the right was Ronald Reagan, once a film actor and, more recently, Governor of California. It was a close contest that highlighted the divisions in the party. The result was uncertain all through the first part of the year, down to the convention itself, which produced a victory for Ford by the narrow margin of 1187 to 1070. The Democrats had chosen Jimmy Carter, the former Governor of Georgia, who had been campaigning doggedly for the nomination for the best part of two years.

In July 1976 the United States celebrated the bicentennial of its independence from Britain. Ford was able to project himself as a national father figure and the glow engendered by the event helped his standing in the opinion polls; but Carter, the fresh face, was still ahead when the campaign began in earnest in September. Ford decided to try to close the gap by challenging him to a series of televised debates, hoping to exploit the Democrat's inexperience of high office. Honours in the debates were roughly even until Ford made a hash of a reply to a question about Eastern Europe. He was asked whether the agreements reached at the Helsinki conference did not amount to a *de facto* recognition of Soviet domination of the Warsaw Pact countries. He replied: 'There is no Soviet domination of Eastern Europe.' He went on to say that the Yugoslavs, Romanians and Poles did not consider themselves dominated by the Soviet Union, and the United States did not concede it.

It was easy to understand what he meant to say – that in the American view the state of affairs in Eastern Europe was temporary. But it was also easy to present it as yet another gaffe by a President out of touch with reality. It was all of a piece with his reputation for clumsiness. His two retractions did not help matters much. As the election approached, however, the gap between the two candidates narrowed as the Republicans pressed their point about Carter's lack of experience. Carter's prospects were also damaged by the third-party candidacy of Eugene McCarthy who, although he polled less than one per cent of the vote nationally, helped Ford win in one or two marginal states. But none of it was quite enough. Carter won a close election with a fraction more of the popular vote than Ford – 40,828,929 to 39,148,940 – and with 297 college delegates to Ford's 241. Ford had to vacate the White House less than three years after moving in – the only incumbent never to have been elected either to the presidency or the vice-presidency.

James E. Carter, 1977–81

Carter's victory was a triumph for thorough, long-term campaigning. He had declared himself a candidate at the end of 1974, nearly two years before the election, and had assiduously built the skeleton of a campaign organisation in all the primary states. By the time of the convention in July, he had enough delegate votes to assure his nomination. He won the election because he projected himself as a Washington outsider – as he was – untainted by the scandals that had shaken the city since the last election. He developed a populist, almost folksy attitude to his high office, making much of his past as a peanut-farmer in Plains, Georgia. Visitors to the White House for a working lunch were surprised – and some of them upset – to be offered hamburgers.

A devout Southern Baptist, he was a more profoundly religious man than most of his recent predecessors. His sister, Ruth, was an evangelist. His mother, Miss Lillian, was often in the news, and he encouraged it. At the time of his inauguration, instead of driving the mile from the Capitol to the White House in the traditional manner, he and his wife Rosalynn walked. And he reinstated the Franklin Roosevelt institution of 'fireside chats' to the nation on television. (Roosevelt's, of course, were on the radio.)

The first mishap to befall the Carter presidency was the Bert Lance affair. Lance was a country banker in Georgia and a former colleague of Carter's in the state administration. Carter had invited him to Washington to take charge of his

Office of Management and Budget – a vital financial position. In the summer of 1977 press reports began to appear alleging that Lance had been involved in improprieties in the banks he ran. A lot of it was to do with the traditionally informal ways of banking in the south. After several inquiries, no specific acts of dishonesty were pinned on to Lance but, in the post-Watergate mood, the press would not let go of the story and in September he resigned.

Carter showed a refreshing enthusiasm for getting to grips with tricky problems. For years the status of the Canal Zone in Panama had been the subject of dispute between the Panamanians and the United States. Since the canal was built in the early years of the century, the US had exercised effective control over the zone. President Johnson had made a commitment to negotiate a new treaty but it was always shelved because of determined opposition from right-wingers in the Senate, whose view was that because the United States had built the canal, it was a matter of national pride as well as security that they should keep control over it and its hinterland for ever.

One of Carter's first foreign policy acts was to launch negotiations on a treaty that would give the Panamanians eventual sovereignty over the Canal, while letting the United States keep permanent rights to use it and to defend it against outside aggression. The negotiations with Panama were tough enough, but the fight to get the treaty through Congress was tougher still. The lobbying campaign went on for months until the two treaties were ratified in the Senate by just one more than the necessary two-thirds majority – a considerable feat of persuasion by the new President to rescue what had once looked like a lost cause.

A second overseas issue that occupied a great deal of the early part of his term was the Middle East. It was only four years since the 1973 war there and tensions and suspicions were still high. Israel was occupying former Arab territories on the west bank of the Jordan and the Sinai peninsula. Egypt and the other nations would not countenance peace talks unless Israel recognised a role for the Palestine Liberation

Organisation. The problem seemed intractable but the role of peacemaker appealed to Carter and he decided to undertake what was in effect a personal peace initiative. He invited President Sadat of Egypt and Prime Minister Begin of Israel on separate visits to Washington. With Carter acting as a broker, the two men began bilateral discussions. Sadat made an historic visit to Jerusalem in November 1977. Negotiations were sticky but the situation looked promising enough for Carter to arrange a meeting between the two leaders at the presidential retreat at Camp David, Maryland, in September 1978, where he would attempt the role of mediator.

The thirteen-day meeting had been on the brink of breakdown numerous times, but at the end of it the three leaders signed two frameworks for Middle East peace agreements. The following March a treaty was signed between Israel and Egypt, and Begin visited Cairo. With other Arab nations disowning the treaty, tensions and violence in the area continued. Sadat was himself assassinated in 1981. All the same, Carter's bold initiative had succeeded in bringing about a measure of friendship between two countries that had historically been at each other's throats. It was an unusual role for an American President but an honourable one.

Before the Israel–Egypt treaty was signed, another event occurred in the Middle East that would cloud the second half of Carter's term and render his re-election impossible. On 16 January the Shah of Iran, a staunch ally of the United States, was forced to leave his country in response to internal pressures. Two weeks later the Ayatollah Khomeini returned from exile in France to establish a revolutionary government.

When it was clear that the Shah would not be able to return to Iran, many of his friends urged Carter to allow him into America. The President was reluctant because the US embassy in Tehran was reporting the danger of reprisals by the Iranians. They wanted the Shah to return to face trial and to give back the fortune they said he had taken with him. In October, the former ruler became ill with cancer and Carter gave permission for him to enter the United States for treatment at a hospital in New York.

Two weeks later, on 4 November 1979, several thousand demonstrators overran the US embassy in Tehran and kidnapped the sixty-five American diplomats working there. The thirteen women and black men among them were released after two weeks. As weeks and then months passed without the release of the others, they became Carter's main preoccupation. He cancelled most of his planned trips out of Washington, although it was the beginning of the election year and he was facing a serious-looking challenge from Senator Edward Kennedy.

The Iranians were now suggesting that the Shah be exchanged for the hostages, but Carter would not countenance that. Instead, the Shah went to Panama. Carter announced a series of economic sanctions, including the freezing of Iranian assets in America. But no pressure worked, chiefly because the hostages were under the control of the revolutionary guard rather than the Iranian government. In April Carter approved a daring rescue mission but it had to be aborted when a dust storm incapacitated some of the helicopters.

A failed rescue is worse than no rescue at all. Because of the Iranians' anger at the attempt, the hostages probably spent longer in custody than they otherwise would have done. But had the rescue succeeded, Carter's reputation would have soared and he would probably have won the 1980 election.

Meantime another foreign issue, of broader significance, demanded his attention. In the last days of 1979 Soviet troops moved into Afghanistan to protect a pro-Soviet government under threat from dissidents. Carter protested vigorously and initiated a series of gestures aimed at signifying US disapproval of the incursion. First, in the face of opposition from farmers and their congressional representatives, he placed an embargo on supplying grain to the Soviet Union: the Russians had suffered from a poor harvest and needed to import grain in quantity. Then he announced a US boycott of the 1980 Olympic Games in Moscow, a gesture that received more general support.

In the first of the primary elections, in New Hampshire, the President had a ten per cent margin over his only serious contender for the nomination, Senator Edward Kennedy, who had gravely damaged his chances in a television interview where he gave inadequate answers to questions about the accident at the Massachusetts island of Chappaquiddick in 1969, when a young woman drowned after a car he was driving plunged from a narrow bridge. He never explained satisfactorily why they were in the car at that remote spot, or his actions immediately afterwards. Carter stayed ahead through most of the primaries and was nominated at the August convention. His opponent was Ronald Reagan, the former Governor of California, who had narrowly failed to win the nomination from President Ford in 1976.

Had the hostages been freed before the 1980 election, the result might have been different, but Carter's failure to secure their release outweighed, in the mind of the electorate, his foreign policy successes. Reagan beat him overwhelmingly, Carter winning in only six states and the District of Columbia. Throughout the remainder of his term he continued to negotiate for the release of the hostages, who finally left Iran on 20 January 1981, the very day he handed over his office to Ronald Reagan.

Ronald W. Reagan, 1981–89

At sixty-nine, Reagan was the oldest man ever to be elected President. His dark black hair, his obvious vigour, his Hollywood charm and his taste for outdoor activities helped people to disregard his age. But just ten weeks after his term began it almost came to a summary end: he was shot in the stomach as he was leaving a Washington hotel. It was painful but, by a near-miracle, little irreparable damage was done and within weeks Reagan was back at his White House desk: a tribute to his cast-iron constitution.

The theme of his campaign had been less government. He wanted to cut the federal bureaucracy and reduce taxes with the money saved. Taxes did go down, the recession of the 1970s came to an end and a long bull market got under way in

1982. For a while there was a sense of prosperity and comparative peace – but federal spending had not been cut sufficiently to prevent a substantial budget deficit, which stored up trouble for his second term. Even before the end of his first term it was apparent that his economic policy was in trouble, but his ease of manner and his (for a politician) unusually sunny personality sustained his popularity. It was a welcome contrast to Carter's pious, brooding intensity. Reagan became known as 'the great communicator'. This quality ensured that he had no difficulty in winning re-election in 1984, when his Democratic opponent, the lacklustre Walter Mondale, won only the District of Columbia and his home state of Minnesota.

Reagan's summit meetings with Mikhail Gorbachev, the new reforming Soviet leader, were cordial enough but achieved comparatively little of substance except a painfully wrought agreement to limit the numbers and locations of medium-range nuclear weapons. In other overseas matters his policy was consistent with the conservatism he espoused before going to the White House. He persuaded a reluctant Congress to approve US aid for the right-wing Contra guerrillas trying to overthrow the left-leaning Sandinista government in Nicaragua. Reagan and his followers saw this as an affirmation of resistance to communism in the western hemisphere, a key test of commitment to the American way of life. But many members of the Democrat-controlled Congress had doubts whether a government that sternly opposed terrorism elsewhere ought to be assisting a band of rebels in overthrowing a legitimate government, even a communist one. There was resistance to authorising further aid.

That was a contributory factor to the scandal in Reagan's second term that harmed him nearly as much as the Watergate affair damaged Nixon, although he avoided the ultimate indignity of being forced to resign. The Iran-Contra affair began near the end of his first term, in 1984, when members of his security staff reached the conclusion that it would be in the interest of the United States to improve relations with Iran. There were two main reasons: to prevent the Russians gaining a dominant position there and to try to exert influence on the Iranians for the release of hostages held in Beirut by men known to be strongly under the influence of Tehran. One way of regaining a foothold in Iran was to supply some of the arms the Iranians needed in order to pursue the war against Iraq that they had been fighting since 1980. Under the Shah, the armed forces had bought chiefly American equipment. Now many of their aircraft and tanks needed American spares which manufacturers could not sell them because of the arms embargo imposed after the 1980 hostage crisis.

Because of Iran's involvement in Middle East terrorism, there was scant prospect of sales of arms to that country being approved by Congress. So members of the National Security Commission, led and motivated by a gung-ho marine lieutenant-colonel named Oliver North, began making secret contact with the Iranians, through suspect intermediaries, arranging covert arms supplies via Israel in exchange for the release of some American hostages. Despite mistrust on both sides, some arms were delivered and some hostages released.

North was among those of Reagan's advisers most passionately committed to the cause of the Contras in Nicaragua and he enthusiastically embraced the idea – whose origins are uncertain – that the profits made on the Iranian arms sales should go to financing the Contra cause, even though Congress was refusing to vote further funds for that purpose. In the autumn of 1986 a Middle East newspaper revealed the arms sales to Iran, and the first reports about the Contra link were published in Washington a few days later. North and Admiral John Poindexter, head of the National Security Commission, resigned, and so did a number of senior White House staff.

Several investigations, formal and informal, failed to establish how far the President himself was involved in all this. It was certain that he had approved the Iranian part of the operation, in a secret presidential 'finding' in January 1986. It was never proved beyond any doubt that he knew about the diversion of funds to the Contras but either way the affair damaged him grievously. If he knew, it meant that he had, like Nixon, grown over-confident, too certain that his view of the world was the right one, convinced that because of his evident popularity he was justified in over-riding constitutional limits to his authority and doing what he thought had to be done – the imperial presidency again.

On the other hand, if he did not know all the details of what North was doing, it implied that he presided over an anarchic White House with no proper lines of authority. At seventy-five, he was beginning to look less and less capable of doing the job. A series of minor operations for skin cancer on his nose provoked worries about whether he was well enough to carry on. The age factor was coming into play at last. One of his former aides wrote in a book that, when associates went to the White House to get decisions on vital matters, they would find Reagan not wrapped in affairs of state, but giving his dog lessons in obedience.

The impression of an ineffectual presidency was enhanced in October 1987 when the most serious stock market crash since 1929 provoked something close to panic around the Western world. It was widely agreed that an important contributory factor was the continuing US budget deficit, but for a long time Reagan stubbornly set his face against reducing it in the most obvious way, by increasing taxes. When he did approve a packet of measures it was seen as inadequate.

His prestige was further dented when he failed to get approval for two nominees in succession to the Supreme Court – one because of his conservative record (the Democrats had won control of the Senate a year earlier) and one because of revelations that he had smoked marijuana in his youth. Reagan pulled back some lost ground at the Washington summit in December 1987 by signing an agreement with the Russians limiting medium-range nuclear weapons. But that did little to allay the widespread feeling that his presidency had lasted at least two years too long. By 1988 a new incumbent at the White House was eagerly awaited and badly needed.

3

The Long Road to the White House

Election day for most public offices in America is the Tuesday following the first Monday in November. (In other words, if 1 November happens to fall on a Tuesday, as in 1988, the election is held on 8 November.) The House of Representatives and a third of the Senate are elected every two years, in years with even dates. The President is elected every four years, when the year is exactly divisible by four – in other words in leap years. His term of office begins at noon on 20 January following the election.

Under the Constitution, the President must be at least thirty-five years old, an American citizen born in the United States and resident there for at least fourteen years. Women, blacks and Jews are not disqualified from the office, although none has ever held it. Every citizen of the United States over eighteen years old is entitled to vote, so long as they are registered, but nearly a third of the voting-age population do not bother to register. Those that do register may do so as supporters of one of the major parties, or as independents. Some states restrict voting in primaries to people who have registered for a particular party. There are always more registered Democrats than Republicans but that is never a reliable guide to individual contests, especially not the presidency. Four of the last five presidential elections have been won by Republicans.

Women have had the franchise since 1920 and black people have theoretically been entitled to vote since the Civil War. But several states placed barriers on black registration until these were outlawed in President Johnson's Voting Rights Act of 1965. In twenty states a literacy test is imposed as a condition for registration and in Alabama potential voters have to take an anti-communist oath. Most states bar convicts from voting.

Anyone born in the US or its territories (Guam, Puerto Rico, American Samoa and US Virgin Islands) has the right to be a citizen, as well as many people born to US citizens temporarily out of the country. Citizenship can also be acquired by people born to other nationalities if they are prepared to give up their former citizenship and they fulfil residency requirements.

Primaries

From the 1830s the parties had chosen their presidential candidates at nominating conventions, but until the beginning of this century delegates to the conventions had been selected by party activists, rather as delegates to party conferences are in Britain. This gave rise to allegations of 'bossism', of manipulation of the conventions by a small group of highly motivated and occasionally corrupt politicians. It also provoked disputes between factions as to which had the right to be represented at the convention. Sometimes two rival sets of delegates would arrive from the same state, and the conventions would begin with heated discussions about which had the right to be seated. Often the eventual choice of candidate would hinge on the decisions of the credentials committee.

At the turn of the century, with the United States going through one of its periodic phases of political reform, pressure grew for a more democratic way of selecting delegates and, by extension, of choosing presidential candidates. Some states were already holding primary elections to select candidates for office in the state legislature. Florida in 1901 and Wisconsin in 1905 were the first two to pass laws authorising primaries to allow supporters of either of the main parties to choose their party's delegates to the national conventions. In neither case did the names of the presidential candidates themselves appear on the ballot papers: voters were assumed to know where the aspiring delegates stood on that critical question, or to trust them to make a judicious choice.

In 1910 the system was refined in Oregon, which became the first state to introduce a presidential preference primary. Here, party supporters voted directly for their choice of the party's candidate for President. Delegates to the conventions would be bound to support the candidate who had come top of the poll, at least in the first ballot at the convention or until the candidate released them from that obligation. The system was at first greeted with enthusiasm and by 1916 more than half of the states – twenty-six – had legislated either for delegate selection primaries or direct preference primaries.

But the limitations of the system soon became apparent, when it was found that success in the primaries did not necessarily mean nomination by the convention. Some eventual nominees had not bothered to enter more than one or two primaries, knowing that the real power still lay in the hands of the party bosses at the conventions. The trouble was that the results of the primaries seldom showed a consistent pattern. Too often victory would go to 'favourite son' candidates who would win only in their own states. This meant that their state delegates were obliged to vote for their favourite son on the first ballot, although he had no chance of the nomination. He would then release them from that obligation and in succeeding ballots their votes were up for grabs, by the traditional method of striking deals in smoke-filled rooms. This was why many ballots were sometimes required before a candidate was selected – the record being 103, when John Davis was chosen by the Democrats in 1924.

Primaries began to come back into favour after World War Two. Eisenhower established his chances early in 1952 by winning the New Hampshire Republican primary. In 1960 John Kennedy had to show that a Catholic could win votes in all parts of the country, and his strong showing in early primaries forced the withdrawal of his main rival, Hubert Humphrey. In 1968 Eugene McCarthy established himself as a viable candidate by winning 41.9 per cent of the vote in New

Hampshire, against 47.6 per cent for President Johnson, who withdrew from the race soon afterwards.

McCarthy's New Hampshire success illustrated an important truth about primaries: the actual ballot result is less important than the performance of the candidate by comparison with what is expected of him. It would have been easy to represent New Hampshire as a triumph for Johnson, for his name had not appeared on the ballot paper and his supporters had to write it in. Moreover, he was receiving much criticism for his policy of bombing North Vietnam. But no opinion polls or press predictions had given McCarthy anything like 40 per cent of the vote. His surprisingly good showing gave his campaign the impetus that carried it through until the convention – although it did not prevent the party establishment ultimately getting its way with the nomination of Hubert Humphrey, who had not entered any primaries at all.

The 1968 campaign for the nomination, culminating in the riots at the Chicago convention, convinced the Democratic Party that changes were needed in the nominating process to give rank-and-file members a better chance of influencing the final choice. The reforms made some kind of democratic consultation compulsory in every state sending delegates to the convention, and the results of the primaries (or caucuses) would be binding on the first ballot. In part this was a reflection of the decline of the old-time party, whose power was largely based on the control of patronage jobs, and therefore waned when such jobs dwindled.

The reforms encouraged more state Democratic parties to hold primaries – and the Republicans felt obliged to follow suit, to prevent their opponents hogging the limelight. Only seventeen primaries had been held in 1968, but by 1980 there were thirty-seven – the same number as in 1988. As a result of this the primary season was extended to begin earlier in the year. To keep its traditional status as the first primary state, New Hampshire was forced in 1976 to move its primary from March to February. Although one of the smallest states it remains one of the most influential and since 1952 nobody has become President without winning the New Hampshire primary.

The earliest primaries and caucuses exert an influence on the selection process out of proportion to the number of delegates chosen at them. In 1987 Dr William Adams, a political science professor at George Washington University, published the results of his analysis of press and television coverage of the 1984 primary season. He found that New Hampshire and Iowa, two states with a low population, received the most attention. Together with New York and California, they commanded more than half of all primary coverage.

In 1984 the Democrats adjusted their system once again to place slightly less power in the hands of elected convention delegates by creating more seats for central party officials. The number of primary states then went down to thirty-one; but it still meant that the majority of the delegates at the convention would be committed in advance to voting in accordance with the primary result in their state. All candidates, therefore, would have to campaign in the primaries to have a realistic hope of winning the nomination. Humphrey's tactic of 1968 could not be repeated: the days appeared to be gone when a contender could sit out the first few primaries, presenting himself at a late stage when his rivals were exhausted through conflict.

The conduct of primaries varies from state to state and between the parties. In some, only voters registered with a party can vote in its primaries. Others allow those registered as independents to vote as well and others hold 'open' primaries in which all registered electors can vote in whichever primary they like.

How delegates are allocated between the candidates, following the primary vote, also varies. Most state Republican parties still retain the winner-take-all system, where the leading candidate wins the loyalty of all that state's convention delegates. Most Democratic parties have some form of proportional representation, with the delegates divided between the candidates in relation to the votes each receives.

The effect of this is to keep more candidates in the hunt for a longer time, as each is likely to pick up a few delegates in all the primaries. A variation of proportional representation is selection by congressional district, where each district of the state is treated as a separate constituency and the delegates for that district are chosen on a winner-take-all system. Three large state Democratic parties that use that system are Illinois, New Jersey and Pennsylvania.

There are also differences in the procedure by which candidates get on the ballot. In some states, officials draw up a list of known contenders and place their names on the ballot paper, either with or without their consent. In others it is up to the candidates to enter themselves for the contest, or to get themselves formally nominated by the requisite number of party members – which means that they must have at least the skeleton of an organisation in those states before they begin campaigning.

Caucuses

This is the oldest method of choosing convention delegates, still practised in a minority of states. The first and best-known is in Iowa, which wins a disproportionate amount of publicity because its final stage traditionally occurs a week before the first primary in February and can influence the course of the campaign. After Christmas the many hundreds of press and television reporters who will follow the candidates around for the next nine months make for Iowa to buttonhole any of the state's 2,800,000 people and ask their political views. Iowans appear to enjoy the brief limelight and for the rest of the nation it marks the ritual start of the democratic process. It was the place where Jimmy Carter began to emerge from the pack of Democrats in 1976, showing he could make a showing elsewhere than in the south. Walter Mondale used the Iowa and other caucuses to great effect in 1984, when about a third of the Democratic convention delegates were elected through caucuses, and more than a quarter of the Republicans.

Caucuses are a series of meetings of party members at various levels, upwards from the precinct – the smallest unit of political organisation, equivalent to a ward in British local politics. At precinct meetings of rank-and-file members, delegates are chosen to attend a county caucus and then a statewide convention to choose members of the state's delegation to the national convention. Although theoretically any registered party supporter can attend these precinct meetings, in practice turnout is much lower than the average at primary elections.

Although the Democratic rule changes after 1968 sought to open up the caucus process to the rank and file, in practice the people who do attend the precinct meeting are still predominantly the political activists. (By Democratic rules they must all be registered supporters but in some states the Republicans allow supporters of other parties to participate in their caucuses as well.) The best way for candidates to campaign is to appear before small groups of party members right across the state, an exhausting and time-consuming business. Statewide advertising and major public speeches are wasteful because they reach too many people who take no part in the caucuses.

Staking claims

Jimmy Carter was the first to recognise that the Democrats' post-1968 procedures put a premium on saturation campaigning in all the primary and caucus states. He announced his candidacy for 1976 at the end of 1974, more than a year before the first primary. He had already been assiduous in making himself known across the nation in advance of his official declaration, recognising the modern truth that the next presidential campaign begins as soon as the last one is over. By the first week of May, 1976, Carter had come first in ten of the eleven Democratic primaries so far contested and his position was effectively unassailable. In 1984 Gary Hart established himself as a viable contender by a strong showing in early primaries, although Walter Mondale was in the end able to rally his forces and head off his previously unconsidered opponent.

In 1988 most primaries were held early in the spring, when it was thought their impact on the final selection would be greater. In 1972 only two primaries had been held by mid-March, while in 1988 there were twenty – more than half the total – completed by then. One key date was 8 March, 'Super Tuesday', when sixteen states, mostly in the south, held their primaries on the same day. On that one day, thirty-seven per cent of the candidates at the Democratic convention were chosen, and a slightly smaller percentage of Republicans. This was a new event on the electoral calendar, initiated by southern Democrats to give them greater influence over the party's nomination at an early stage in the campaign (see page 190). It might not be repeated next time.

The modern pattern is for the field of candidates to start forming some two years in advance of the election. There can be as many as a dozen live contenders for each party – unless, as in 1984, a popular incumbent President seeks a second term, when his nomination is usually more or less automatic. In time some drop out, either because of poor poll ratings and consequent lack of financial support, or because of some slip-up or scandal (e.g. Biden and Hart for the Democrats in 1987, although Hart later re-entered the lists – see page 178).

By the beginning of election year the field has usually been whittled down to three or four on each side at the most, although the Democrats in 1988 were an exception to that rule. This is the point at which the Secret Service offers its protection to the leading contenders – a potent symbol that the campaign is getting serious in one of the world's largest democracies, and one of its most dangerous.

A better way?

The object of both the primary and caucus systems is to give the electors the chance of choosing the candidates from which the final choice of President will be made. This sets the United States apart from most other democracies, where the political parties themselves choose the candidates to put before the people. All the same, fewer than thirty-five million people voted in primaries or at caucuses in 1980 – around forty per cent of the number of voters in the election proper, which was itself only a little more than half the eligible voters. (The 1984 primary voting figure was still lower because President Reagan's nomination as Republican candidate was virtually uncontested.)

One weakness of primaries and caucuses is their haphazard nature, with their conduct varying from state to state. Some critics believe that the number of separate contests an aspirant has to enter discourages the best potential presidents from entering the contest at all. The amount of travelling a candidate must do during the primary season is in itself daunting. With, say, the New Hampshire primary only a week away, the serious candidate ought to be spending most of his time there. But only three weeks later there are primaries in larger states like Florida and Texas, at the other end of the country. Only the airlines really gain from this need for candidates to put in appearances right across the country. Certainly the process weeds out the faint-hearted – but it also might eliminate people who would have made better Presidents.

To avoid these drawbacks, it has been suggested that there should be one national primary to replace the series of state primaries and caucuses. This would curtail the campaign season and cut its cost, reduce the strain on the participants and lessen the advantage held by contenders prepared to subject themselves to relentless media exposure for up to two years. Yet there are two main drawbacks to this superficially sensible suggestion which make it unlikely that it will be adopted. First, it would reduce the input of the individual states into the nomination process and would thus be opposed by enthusiasts for states' rights. Secondly, it would so downgrade the function of the party conventions – the traditional highlights of a presidential election year – that it would scarcely be worth holding them.

A less radical proposal is for a series of regional primaries – say half a dozen – to replace the present state by state voting. 'Super Tuesday' represents an informal move towards this, but it has spawned no imitators so far.

The campaign team

Well before they make the formal announcements of their candidacy, the hopefuls try to recruit good and experienced staff. It is a competitive undertaking. The political advisers, opinion pollsters, fund raisers and image-creators with the best track records are much in demand. And they have become nationally-known characters, for the political reporters find them as fascinating as the candidates themselves. The four key positions to fill are campaign director, research director, finance director and media director. Together, they decide on the nature of the appeal the candidate will make to voters – the sales pitch – and they shape the campaign accordingly.

Sometimes the key advisers are people who have known the candidate for years and performed the same service in state elections earlier – men like Hamilton Jordan and Gerald Rafshoon, who master-minded President Carter's campaigns. Most, though, are freelancers who make a career out of handling a variety of candidates in city, state and national elections. The best known is David Garth, responsible for turning an amiable New Yorker named Mario Cuomo from a failed candidate for mayor into a popular state governor and then into the reluctant but much-courted candidate for the Democratic presidential nomination.

These professionals now have much more influence on the campaign than the hard-bitten old politicians who used to 'run' their candidates by making deals to win the support of local party machines. Under the guidance of the new experts, detailed market research is applied to the electorate. A candidate's image and his pledges will generally be tailored to fit what the research shows the public want, rather than reflecting any deeply-held political conviction. As a result, the winning candidate's election promises often bear scant relation to what he does in office.

The new breed of senior advisers are paid; and paid handsomely. Lowlier campaign workers are either seconded by sympathetic employers or do it for nothing, in the hope of establishing links that might help their own political careers in the future. Local politicians, especially those up for election or re-election on the same day as the President, will usually give their support to the candidate they judge to have the best chance of helping their own cause by attracting votes for the party and thus for them – the so-called 'coat-tails effect'. That is why it is far easier for a candidate doing well in the opinion polls to recruit helpers. By the time a successful candidate has won the nomination, his campaign staff could number 500.

The direct approach

Another method of gleaning and gauging support, and of raising funds, is also derived from the techniques of commercial marketing. Scores of people, either volunteers or paid helpers, sit at banks of telephones, on which they contact individual voters in the primary states. The practise of telephoning people out of the blue and asking them to buy something is an effective though labour-intensive method of marketing. In a primary election or caucus, where turnout is often low, it can make all the difference. Sometimes the candidate himself comes on the 'phone to talk to potential backers. The 'phone banks also provide a way of monitoring public reaction to the candidate's latest speech or television appearance.

Even if the telephone personnel are not being paid, the installation of the system is costly. Most candidates could not afford it until the advent of federal matching funds (see page 88), but today a telephone bank is a vital tool for anyone seriously running for his party's presidential nomination.

Happy families

It is sexist but true that a loyal wife, or at least one who can be made to seem loyal in public, is an essential prerequisite nowadays for a candidate for President. Only one bachelor has been elected to the White House – James Buchanan in 1856 – although there have been several widowers. When Jerry Brown, Governor of California, entered the lists for the Democratic nomination in 1980, his publicists stressed his close friendship with the singer Linda Ronstadt, hinting that marriage could be in the air. (It wasn't.) Suggestions of marital infidelity can destroy a campaign, as Edward Kennedy, still under the cloud of Chappaquiddick, found in 1980, and Gary Hart in 1988.

A wife's role in a campaign is a delicate one. She has to be charming, alert and endlessly supportive without, in today's climate, seeming over-subservient to her husband. Naturally, she campaigns chiefly among women's groups and devotes any speeches mainly to domestic concerns rather than portentous discussions of national and international policy. Their children, if old enough, are also expected to lend support, dropping any professional activities for the duration of the campaign. In the campaigns of John Kennedy and Jimmy Carter, other relatives were also roped in.

Once her husband is elected, the wife's task is to forge a role for herself independent of the presidency but not in conflict with it. Of recent First Ladies, Rosalynn Carter has perhaps carried it off best, involving herself energetically with a government inquiry into mental health while supporting her husband with dedication over the Iran hostages and other crises. Nancy Reagan won a reputation for wielding excessive influence over her husband, especially in his choice of advisers. The stories may have been exaggerated but they were damaging to an ageing President already suspected of not devoting sufficient energy to the job.

Opinion polls

Since 1920, when the magazine *Literary Digest* first asked its readers to return a coupon saying how they would vote, opinion polling techniques have been refined. The polls now play a critical role at all stages of the campaign. As the importance of the primaries and caucuses has increased, so has the significance of the burgeoning polls that sample the attitudes and preferences of the electorate in minute detail at ever more frequent intervals. They amount effectively to a permanent taking of the national pulse. Apart from those published in newspapers, magazines and on television, candidates commission polls of their own from one of the numerous polling organisations, or they may even have a full-time pollster on the campaign staff. They and their advisers study the polls in obsessive detail and use them in a variety of ways.

Good poll ratings can mean healthy financial contributions and make it easier to recruit good campaign staff. Conversely a candidate who persistently performs badly in the polls quits the contest sooner than he would have done in the days before he had that means of knowing how badly he was doing.

Polls are analysed not just for the crude figures of comparative support for each candidate. Like the primary results themselves, they can be used to measure the crucial element of impetus. Thus if a poll shows a candidate's support at just two per cent one month, four per cent the next month and eight per cent the month after, a bandwagon effect is detected. This is reported enthusiastically in the press and can be exploited by the campaign workers to attract more backing. Similarly, if a candidate does significantly better in the primary than in the preceding opinion polls, that can be seen as evidence that he attracts support where it counts, at the ballot box, and can again be used to start the bandwagon rolling. The converse is also true: a candidate who does worse than the polls suggest, even if he still comes out on top, can be on the slide.

In national elections, opinion poll figures based on sufficiently large samples are usually reflected broadly by actual voting results, but not always. The most famous exception was in the 1948 election, where President Truman beat Thomas Dewey soundly, despite the near-unanimous verdict of the pollsters that the Republican would defeat the incumbent. Such inaccuracies can be caused by errors in sampling or by the volatility of voters, who may respond to some late development in the campaign by changing their minds at the last minute. Paradoxically, the polls themselves may sometimes contribute to such eleventh-hour switching. (For exit polls, see page 101).

Campaign financing

Important reforms to methods of financing presidential elections were introduced in 1974 in the wake of the Watergate affair. The investigations into the scandal and its ramifications uncovered some serious financial abuses. Large donations from important corporations were passed through several secret accounts to the Committee to Re-Elect the President (CREEP), which had organised the Watergate burglary of Democratic Party headquarters. It was disclosed, for instance, that a large hotel chain, part of a multi-national conglomerate, had donated valuable facilities to the Republican convention in San Diego, at a time when the parent company needed the administration's support in an anti-trust case.

That was not an isolated example. It differed from standard practice in presidential campaigns only by dint of its scale and its blatant nature. Before the reforms, a candidate had to raise his own money for the campaign, sometimes (although rarely in modern times) from his personal fortune or more often through donations from big business. To raise money from business a candidate had first and foremost to make a convincing case that he was likely to win. Nobody is going to lay out significant funds unless there is a real prospect of being able to recoup a dividend in the shape of ready access to the seat of power and the ability to lobby for legislation that will protect the company's interests.

One of the last presidential contenders to succeed by dint of his personal fortune was John Kennedy in 1960. Because he was backed by a wealthy family he was not obliged to make as many concessions to big business as was customary. It is ironic that his liberal reputation stems largely from his having access to a substantial private fortune. For the most part, however, it was the Republicans – long the favourite party of Wall Street and the business community – who benefited from the lack of control over campaign donations.

The Federal Elections Act of 1974 introduced government financing for the primary campaigns, the national convention and the presidential campaign itself. In the case of the primaries the federal money is in the form of matching funds. Candidates have to demonstrate broad national support to qualify. They have to raise at least $100,000 on their own, in the form of $5,000 from each of twenty states. No individual contribution may exceed $1,000 and only the first $250 of each donation qualifies for matching funds, which means that to get maximum government backing an aspirant must attract many small-scale supporters, rather than a few large ones. Sophisticated direct mail fund-raising techniques have been evolved to achieve this. If they receive enough small contributions, the candidates can garner up to $5 million in matching funds, so long as no one candidate receives more than twenty-five per cent (and no party more than forty-five per cent) of the total distributed.

To qualify for federal funds in 1988 the candidate had to limit his spending on the primaries to around $27m, divided between the states on the basis of how many eligible voters are registered in each state. Nor must contenders spend more than $50,000 of their own money. Spending limits also apply to the presidential campaign itself once the candidates have been selected. The two main parties get $9 million federal funds each for their conventions and $46.75 million for the campaign. If they choose to spend more than that they forfeit all federal funds and must finance their entire campaign from their supporters' resources. No party or candidate has chosen this course since the federal funding option was introduced.

Large contributions from companies or individuals, paid directly to a candidate, are banned, but instead donations may be made to political action committees (PACs) established by supporters. No PAC may contribute more than $5,000 to a campaign but there is no limit to the number of PACs that can be formed. Donations from PACs do not qualify for federal matching funds.

The limits on expenditure have helped change the nature of campaigning. With resources having to be husbanded carefully, expenditure on fripperies such as campaign hats, lapel buttons, balloons and bumper stickers has decreased so that more money can be poured into the really vital medium, television. In theory the new laws should help the Democrats, who customarily find it harder to raise private donations than the Republicans. But of the three presidential elections held since the restrictions came into effect, the Republicans, in the person of Ronald Reagan, have won twice.

Campaigning: on the stump

Until midway through the nineteenth century it was thought immodest, not to say improper, for candidates actively to solicit votes on their own behalf, although their supporters would sometimes arrange parades and demonstrations that set the tone of political campaigning until superseded by mass communications a century later. It is widely accepted that William Henry Harrison in 1840 (see p. 22) engaged in the first presidential election campaign in something like the form in which it later developed, with national tours, personal appearances heralded by brass bands and parades, campaign songs and slogans. In fact Harrison had started touring in his unsuccessful election bid four years earlier, but on a smaller scale. And as early as 1828 campaigners for Andrew Jackson, 'Old Hickory', erected tall hickory poles in town centres as symbols of support for their man.

The phrase 'climbing aboard the bandwagon' derives from these old-style campaigns. In the parades on behalf of the candidates, the brass band would play on the back of a wagon. To signify their support for the candidate, influential local people would climb on to the wagon with the musicians.

Throughout the second half of the nineteenth century, presidential campaigns centred more and more around the personality and magnetism of the contenders. To be a skilled orator became an important attribute. Candidates would travel across the country by train and give speeches at small centres of population from the rear platform of their railway carriages – the origin of the phrase 'whistle-stop tour'. They would deliver speeches tailor-made for the particular locality, sometimes making commitments that were hard to reconcile with one another: a pledge to cut food prices, made in towns, would be reversed in agricultural districts. William Jennings Bryan, the unsuccessful Democratic candidate in 1896, calculated that in a 100-day campaign he travelled 18,000 miles in twenty-seven states and made 600 speeches. In 1940 Wendell Wilkie, the Republican fighting Franklin Roosevelt, covered 30,000 miles, although by this time some of the longer trips were made by air.

Today the candidates travel the length and breadth of the country in chartered jets – but the purpose is different. They are not projecting themselves to a local audience so much as providing a platform for a national appearance. So they have to maintain consistency and refer less to local issues. These televised campaign meetings are hardly ever open to the public. The audiences are made up of reliable supporters of the candidate. Their object is to stage an enthusiastic show of support for their man when the cameras are switched on and the print journalists are in their places.

Radio and television

The immense popularity of radio in the 1920s, and television in the 1950s, changed campaigning styles. Powerful oratory gave way to a more persuasive fireside manner tailored to the intimacy of the new media that penetrated people's homes. The cinema, too, was a place where the simultaneous attention of millions of voters could be grabbed, either through newsreel reporting or short campaign films made by the parties. Here again, the emphasis had to be on intimacy rather than oratory.

From as early as 1940, when there were only a few thousand television sets in the country, the TV cameras were admitted to the party conventions and over the years would come to dominate them by determining their timing, content and character. In 1948, when there was not yet a fully national television network, both parties chose to hold their conventions in Philadelphia, which had a coaxial cable TV link with the main east coast population centres.

By the time of the 1952 campaign the east and west coasts were linked by cable, allowing the creation of national network television. From then on, television became the paramount campaign medium. Candidates hired media advisers, usually with experience in making TV commercials, to ensure that the cameras brought out their best traits and concealed their worst ones. Advertising agencies would be engaged to create the TV campaign – a development at first derided in other countries, including Britain, but later emulated by them. They would buy long spots, up to half an hour, for their candidates to project themselves. Later they decided that the most effective form of advertising was the short commercial lasting around a minute, using the same quick-fire techniques employed in advertising consumer products.

1952 was the first time television had a decisive and definable effect on the course of a campaign. Eisenhower's running-mate for Vice-President, Richard Nixon, had been subjected to attacks from Democratic opponents for accepting money and gifts from wealthy California business people. Nixon defended himself in the renowned 'Checkers speech' in which he presented himself, his family and their pet spaniel Checkers as humble Americans struggling to make ends meet like most of their fellow-citizens. The speech, watched in nearly half the households with television, set the style for television appearances by politicians. Nixon saved his spot on the ticket and probably his political career.

In 1960, the medium that had rescued Nixon eight years earlier played its part in his defeat by John Kennedy. In a televised debate between them, Nixon was shown to have 'five o'clock shadow' around his chin and beads of sweat on his forehead, making him look uncomfortable, even shifty by comparison with the dashing and immaculate Kennedy. Polls showed that this affected viewers' perception of the two men's comparative performances and their fitness to survive the strains of office.

At the start of the 1980 campaign John Kennedy's youngest brother Edward in turn fell foul of the revelatory nature of television. An hour-long profile of him made by the CBS network, which he hoped would launch his bid to wrest the Democratic nomination from the incumbent President, Jimmy Carter, turned into a disaster. Interviewed by Roger Mudd, he gave indecisive answers to such basic questions as why he wanted to be President, and was unconvincing in his explanation of the Chappaquiddick affair (see page 70). His campaign never recovered and Carter had the nomination sewn up through primary victories well before the convention.

The 'character' issue

It was not Kennedy's involvement in the Chappaquiddick incident itself that appeared to count most heavily against him, but his fumbling response to Mudd's far from malevolent questions. It was widely assumed, rightly or wrongly, that the woman passenger who drowned was in his car for immoral reasons, but the electorate seem more broad-minded on such matters than is sometimes assumed. When Gary Hart re-entered the race for the Democratic nomination at the end of 1987, after withdrawing some months earlier following allegations of an extra-marital affair with a model, he immediately shot to the top of the polls, if only temporarily. He had earlier criticised the climate of opinion that had persuaded him to withdraw, pointing out: 'I was not running for sainthood.'

Many voters seemed to agree with him and with the Reverend Henry Ward Beecher, who commented at a rally in 1884 on the sexual smear campaign being waged against Grover Cleveland (see page 31): 'If every man in New York tonight who had broken the seventh commandment voted for Cleveland he would be elected by a 200,000 majority.' Cleveland won, although his majority in New York was much narrower than that.

It is legitimate to expect a potential President to display decisiveness. Kennedy's lack of that important quality in his response to Mudd reminded voters that he had also acted tentatively in the immediate aftermath of the accident. That was the 'character' issue that destroyed him. Similarly with the Democratic candidacy of Senator Joseph Biden, again in 1987. He was forced to withdraw not because he had borrowed passages from the speeches of Neil Kinnock, the British Labour Party leader, but because there appeared to be something a little shifty about the way he had gone about it. Hart, on the other hand, was perceived to have been decisive and honourable by withdrawing from the contest after the allegations against him, and even more decisive in his surprising decision to re-enter it. Moral perfection is not, apparently, one of the qualities the US electorate insist on when weighing up candidates, although it probably helps.

While the fashionable view is to deplore the 'hounding' of candidates about details of their private lives, some believe it a legitimate part of the process of choosing a President. In an interview with the *Observer* in November 1987, Walter Mondale, the defeated Democratic candidate in 1984, said:

Here's someone suddenly announces he's running for President and the American people are desperately anxious to find out whether he's got backbone, brains, values and stamina. That fires up those character questions, which is a cruel way to handle it, but it's my belief that there are no bad questions, only bad answers.

What, then, *are* the qualities people look for? If there were a straightforward answer to that question, we would see a series of Identikit candidates, all fashioned by their image moulders to portray those precise qualities. The mood of the electorate changes and at different times different qualities are sought. In periods of uncertainty Americans have often looked to military men – hence to Eisenhower when the cold war was at its height. As a reaction to eight years of him they sought youth and boldness in Kennedy. After Carter's slightly frenetic presidency they chose Reagan's calm assurance. Define the mood, catch it and you are half-way there.

Debates: one on one

The televised debate between primary contenders and then between the two parties' chosen candidates has become ever more familiar, though in some cases incumbent Presidents refuse to take part in debates during the primaries because they think the exposure will be of greater benefit to their lesser-known opponents. Four debates have been scheduled for the two nominees this year: on 14 September, 25 September, 11 October and 27 October.

The debates are seldom more than stilted and ritualistic, with the candidates giving well-prepared answers to identical questions put by the moderator, and seldom responding directly to each other's points. It is dangerous to be too specific. The object is to convey a general impression of authority and reliability, rather than promote detailed aspects of policy.

An important priority is to avoid an unguarded remark that might give offence to any of the significant national lobby groups – elderly people, women, farmers, gun owners, blacks or other ethnic minorities. President Ford learned that the hard way: his infelicitous remark about Poland in his debate with Jimmy Carter in 1976 offended Jews and immigrants from eastern Europe and may have cost him the election (see page 65). It is usually much more profitable for a candidate to try to manoeuvre his opponent into an error of this kind than to engage in the frank abuse that was a hallmark of campaigns in pre-television days. 'Ford gaffe on Poland' is a much more potent headline than 'Carter calls Ford a know-nothing'. Invective is still sometimes employed, but is nowadays essentially a defensive weapon of last resort for a candidate doing poorly in the opinion polls.

How the press reports the televised debates next morning is vital in determining the public perception of who wins and who loses. Most people prefer to see what the experts say before venturing a verdict of their own. Thus although television is of paramount importance, the written press still has a role in creating the climate of opinion in which a candidate's star is judged as being in the ascendant or on the wane. So a persuasive press officer, skilled in putting the most favourable gloss on primary election or opinion poll results, and on his man's showing in the debates, is a key member of the campaign team.

The boys and girls on the bus

As the primaries progress and one or two candidates emerge from the pack as front runners, the major newspapers, agencies and television networks assign specific reporters to follow the leaders. They travel in the campaign planes and on chartered buses, listening to the same speech dozens of times over, on the watch for the inadvertent slip that could spell disaster. In earlier times they were known as 'the boys on the bus' but today many women are among them.

It is hard in these circumstances for reporters to distance themselves far enough from the campaign to report it objectively, for after a while they become almost a part of the candidate's team, forming friendships with him, his staff and his family. To some extent the reporters attached to a candidate have an interest in his success, because if he wins the nomination they are likely to be given the prestige assignment of reporting his presidential campaign.

In 1988, however, there has been a move away from expensive live coverage of the campaign by all but the largest newspapers. The rest subscribe instead to a service called Presidential Hotline, which gives up-to-date news on all aspects of the campaign, so the stories can be written without reporters having to leave the office. It may lack immediacy but it is very much more economical.

The conventions

These take place in summer at a convention centre in one of the large cities. They last four days. Civic authorities lobby hard for the right to host a convention, which brings in large amounts of revenue and publicity. They will offer money from public or private funds, as well as many free facilities, to influence the parties' choices.

In 1988 both conventions were in the south – the Democrats at Atlanta in July and the Republicans at New Orleans in August. Both parties recognised the importance of the south as the region where the election could well be won and lost. The Democratic event was by far the bigger, with 4,160 delegates to the Republicans' 2,277. The Democratic total included a new category of 643 national 'superdelegates', not chosen by the states but appointed by the central party organisation, with the object of taking some of the nominating power away from local party activists (see page 78). Democratic rules require that state delegations contain an equal number of men and women. The chairmanship also has to alternate between the sexes from one convention to the next.

The increased importance of primaries and caucuses has meant a consequent down-grading of the conventions as places where the key bargains are made and the real selection process takes place. More often than not it is clear who will be the candidate because of the number of pledged votes he brings to the convention with him. (In 1980 supporters of Edward Kennedy tried to change the rules so as not to make it compulsory for delegates to stick to their pledged candidate for the first ballot. The move was defeated, meaning that Jimmy Carter won the nomination automatically.) The importance of the conventions today lies less in the business of candidate selection than in providing four days of saturation television coverage for the party. They are carefully timed and staged with that in mind.

There are often demonstrations for candidates, both for those who have a chance of the nomination and those who have not. These are planned to look spontaneous, with supporters parading in the convention hall with music and razzamatazz at a time calculated to have the maximum impact on the television audience. These manifestations are generally designed to establish a candidate's position for a future race, or for nomination as Vice-President or some other position of influence. Not since 1952, when it took the Democrats three ballots to choose Adlai Stevenson, has either party needed more than one ballot for the selection. Before 1936 the Democrats had a rule that the successful candidate had to receive two-thirds of the vote, which extended the balloting process. Today both parties require only a simple majority.

Many commentators believed that this year's Democratic convention would need more than one ballot and would be the first for some years to be a 'brokered convention'. This view was based on the possibility that the Rev. Jesse Jackson would have most pledged delegates at Atlanta but fewer than half. He would be unlikely to win the nomination but he would be in a strong position to make bargains with other candidates, presumably insisting on an unambiguous civil rights plank in the party platform as a price for his support. This would allow a figure such as Mario Cuomo, who had not entered the primaries, to emerge as the nominee: back to the pre-1968 pattern.

Agreeing the platform is the second most important function of the conventions (after the selection of the candidate) and the one that provokes the most public disagreements. The convention must also formally approve the selection of the candidate for Vice-President, but in practice the man or woman chosen by the presidential nominee is automatically endorsed. The climax of the four days is the acceptance speech by the chosen presidential candidate, although until Franklin Roosevelt's nomination in 1932 it had been customary for the nominee not to appear at the convention.

All to play for

The official start of the campaign is the day after Labor Day, a national holiday celebrated on the first Monday of September, traditionally marking the country's return to business after the summer vacation. In fact, of course, the final eight weeks of campaigning are simply the climax of a process that has been virtually continuous for more than a year. But with the candidates and their running-mates now officially selected, voters can seriously weigh up their respective claims without the confusion engendered by a large field of contenders twelve months earlier.

The techniques of campaigning are the same as those employed in the early part of the year, but more intensive. Public opinion polls come almost daily now, and both sets of candidates can usually find some comfort in them – if not a straight lead, then an improving trend. Seldom does one side hold so commanding a position as to offer the other no hope whatever, because in recent years party loyalties have become much less rigid. Surveys by the University of Michigan Survey Research Center and the University of Chicago National Opinion Research Center show that thirty years ago only nineteen per cent of voters regarded themselves as uncommitted to either of the main parties, compared with thirty-two per cent today.

Most of those who do support one of the major parties plump for the Democrats – forty per cent as against only twenty-seven per cent for the Republicans – but the Republicans often do much better in presidential elections than in local races. With the intense coverage given to the candidates by the media, it becomes a contest of personalities rather than of philosophies. This is one of the factors that has led to the decline of the big-city political machines. Their speciality was getting out the vote for their party. With party loyalties less certain, they might find themselves driving to the polls people who are going to vote for their opponents.

Third-party candidates

There are invariably more than two candidates on the presidential ballot paper. In 1984, for instance, fifteen people were in the field apart from Ronald Reagan and Walter Mondale, although none contested every state and most stood in only a handful. Between them they polled only 0.6 per cent of the vote. The purpose of the candidacies was to give themselves a platform for the promotion of their minority political views, even if they stood little chance of making much impact against the expensive campaigns of the two main parties.

Some third-party candidates do better than that. In 1980 John Anderson, a liberal Republican running as an independent, picked up 6.6 per cent of the popular vote, doing especially well in New England. In 1968 the conservative populist George Wallace polled much better, winning 13.53 per cent of the vote and picking up enough support in the southern states to have forty-six delegates in the electoral college. He probably gained enough Democratic votes in the south to prevent Hubert Humphrey from defeating Richard Nixon. In 1948 Strom Thurmond, campaigning as a States' Rights Democrat, or Dixiecrat, only contested southern states, where he won thirty-nine college delegates. It was expected that his intervention would mean the defeat of President Truman, but Truman won despite him. Although third-party candidates never win, their presence can add an extra element of uncertainty to the outcome in a close contest.

The day arrives

Voting usually takes place in a local school. Election Day is a school holiday across America. At one time many businesses would close too – and so would the bars, a relic of the days when party officers used to try to bribe voters with liquor.

Going into the booth on the Tuesday after the first Monday in November, the voter is given a long list of candidates for various less important elective offices as well as the choice of two or more for President. In most states nowadays voting is by machine: Thomas Edison invented the first one in 1868. Electors can vote in each contest individually, or for the 'slate' of one party or another by pulling just one designated lever. (This explains the importance of the 'coat-tails effect' – see page 197.) Where machines have not been introduced, voters put a cross next to the names of their choices on a ballot paper, in the traditional way.

In some states, notably California, there are also 'propositions' on the ballot. Here, the voters are asked to support or oppose specific items of policy proposed by politicians, endorsed by the required number of the state's residents. The business of voting in the USA is much more elaborate than the usual British system of simply placing a cross against one of a list of candidates.

Turn-out in presidential elections – indeed in American elections of all kinds – is surprisingly low given the intensity of the media coverage, and it has decreased over the years. In 1984 only 92,652,793 voted, or 53.3 per cent of the estimated number of citizens of voting age. This compares with seventy per cent at the turn of the century. The figure, though, is a percentage of the number of people entitled to vote rather than those who have placed themselves on the electoral roll by registering. Part of the reason for the low turn-out is that many citizens – about thirty per cent – do not bother to register, despite official campaigns urging them to do so. Young people between eighteen and twenty-one, given the vote for the first time in 1972, are the most apathetic: fewer than half of them vote.

The candidates and their wives set a good example by casting their votes early in the day, accompanied by scores of cameramen and photographers, to provide material for the evening papers and the early news bulletins. They invariably deliver confident predictions of a famous victory.

Watching and waiting

The polls usually close at 9 p.m. This means that because of the different time zones when voting is finished on the east coast there are still three hours to go on the west. Results start coming in, district by district, very soon after the polls close. Officials do not wait until a whole state's votes are counted before starting to announce the early figures.

All three major US television networks devote themselves entirely to reporting and analysing the results as soon as the first ones come in. They feed the early figures through their computers and predict who will win and by how big a margin. Their prediction, constantly updated as more results are made available, becomes a major news story, but it is not necessarily exact because if there are significant regional variations in voting patterns, the picture might change as the returns come in from the more westerly states. The early results, coming from the big cities of the east, tend to err towards the Democrats. Alongside the presidential returns, the networks also keep viewers up to date with the contests for seats in Congress and in the election of new state governors (see page 196).

One difference between watching election results in Britain and the United States is that in an American presidential election there is no mention of 'swing' from one party to the other. This is because it is so much a matter of personality rather than party loyalty that there is little value in comparing the results with the previous presidential election or the elections for other offices.

In recent years a more accurate forecast of the final figures has come from the 'exit polls' taken from a sample of people as they leave voting stations. Asking people how they *have* voted rather than how they intend to vote provides a more reliable indication than the opinion polls taken in advance of the election. And because samples are taken from all over the country, regional variations in voting can be taken into account. The results of these exit polls are announced as soon as the polling stations close, and the networks generally run them alongside the computer analysis of the actual voting returns, as an alternative basis for prediction.

Politicians from the west coast complain about having a stream of results and forecasts coming in while the polls in their states are still open. They believe that their constituents are persuaded that the contest is already over and it will make no difference how they cast their vote – so they stay at home. This can affect close races for Congress and state governorships being contested at the same time. For this reason some western congressmen introduced legislation to have the poll close at 9 p.m. Eastern Standard Time all across the nation. Because this would mean closing the booths unreasonably early (6 p.m.) in the west, it was further proposed that summer time should remain in force for an extra fortnight after the customary date in the Pacific time zone, so that it would be 7 p.m. and not 6 p.m. when voting ended there. The Senate has still to act on the proposal.

In Britain at least one TV channel is sure to stay open for live satellite coverage of the presidential election results, beginning shortly after 2 a.m. British time. For those who do not want to stay up that late, the breakfast shows – TV-am on the ITV network and *Breakfast Time* on BBC1 – will have complete coverage, some of it live.

Winning and losing gracefully

The point at which the final result becomes clear varies depending how narrow the victory margin is. In the 1960 election it was not certain until Wednesday afternoon that John Kennedy had won. In 1980 President Carter conceded defeat as early as 9.30 Eastern Standard Time – before the polls in the west had closed. Candidates usually spend the evening in hotel suites in their home cities, so that they can easily congratulate or commiserate with their supporters holding a party in the ballroom. Incumbent Presidents customarily stay in the White House and go to a Washington hotel to make their party appearance. When victory for one of the candidates is clear beyond doubt, it is traditional for his opponent to make a graceful concession speech. Then the way is clear for the winner to descend in triumph to the hotel ballroom, where champagne corks pop as he pays tribute to his opponent's campaign and calls for national unity and support from all sections of the population, now that the battle is over.

In a close race, it is theoretically possible for the candidate with most votes overall still to be the loser, because of the rule that the winner in every state gets all that state's electoral votes, regardless of the margin of his victory. Such an unjust result has not occurred since 1888, when Benjamin Harrison won a comfortable majority of sixty-five in the electoral college, while gaining 90,000 fewer votes than Grover Cleveland. In 1960 John Kennedy had a majority of only 115,000 over Richard Nixon in the popular vote, but a college majority of eighty-four.

Because of minority party candidates on the ballot paper (see page 99) it is quite common for the successful candidate to gain fewer than half the total of popular votes: it has happened fifteen times altogether and six times this century. But he has to win an overall majority in the electoral college itself, which today means 270 of the 538 votes there. If no candidate gains an overall majority the election is decided by the House of Representatives, but with each state's members allowed only one vote between them, making fifty-one votes in all (including the District of Columbia). The election has not gone to the House of Representatives since 1824 (see page 20).

Taking over

The two and a half months between the election and the inauguration of the new President – assuming the incumbent has not been re-elected – are an unsatisfactory hiatus in the nation's life. Yet the retiring President has more to do than ruminate over the memories of his term. He has to present a budget for the next financial year. He has to work on his final State of the Union address to Congress, delivered in the week before his departure. He can, and generally does, introduce a sheaf of bills in the so-called 'lame duck' session of Congress. If Congress is controlled by his own party, which may have lost seats at the recent election, then the President's proposals are generally carried. If not, there is no way he can force Congress to toe the line, since there will be no time to call it back into special session, as he is entitled to do earlier in his term.

The newly-elected President forms a 'transition team' to absorb all the background information he will need to do the job and to ensure that he is fully primed for the start of his term on 20 January. Normally his predecessor and the White House staff will give all the help they can, even if the two men have very different political views. In sensitive areas such as foreign affairs and defence, the retiring President will not take binding decisions without the approval of the new one, so as to assure continuity.

The inaugural parade in Washington on 20 January – often held in cold and snowy weather – is generally a time of optimism. The new President takes his 35-word oath of office on a platform outside the Capitol:

I do solemnly swear (or affirm) that I will faithfully execute the office of President of the United States, and will to the best of my ability preserve, protect and defend the Constitution of the United States.

After making a speech in which he attempts to set the tone for his administration, the new President and his wife drive the 1.2 miles from the Capitol to the White House, down wide avenues lined with cheering people. (President Carter and his family walked it, to signify a new presidential style.) They sit in a temporary pavilion outside the White House and review a parade before making their formal entry into their new official home. The day ends with the inaugural ball. Next day the new President begins the toughest four years of his life, during which many of his and his supporters' high hopes are almost certain to be unfulfilled.

The White House

The first Congress, sitting in New York, decided in 1790 to build a new capital away from the main cities of the new Republic, and to name it after the first President. After heated disagreement about the site (northern Congressmen pressed for Germantown, Pennsylvania), it was agreed to place it on the Potomac River border between Maryland and Virginia, on land ceded by the two states. This was roughly in the middle of the Union as it then was. The French architect L'Enfant drew up a plan for a modern city with broad avenues radiating from two central points – the Capitol, where the two houses of Congress would meet, and the President's house, or executive mansion, later known as the White House. A competition was held to find an architect to design the President's house and was won by James Hoban, an Irish immigrant.

John Adams was the first President to occupy the White House, moving there with his wife Abigail in November 1800, when the building works were still unfinished. In 1814 a British invading force sailed up the Potomac and set fire to Washington, including the White House and most of its contents; although Dolley Madison, the President's wife, managed to rescue one of Gilbert Stuart's portraits of George Washington. The British were defeated at New Orleans the following January and the capital was rebuilt, with Hoban supervising the reconstruction of the White House. President

Monroe moved back in 1817 and it has served as the home of US Presidents ever since then.

Over the years it has been enlarged several times but has retained its character as an imposing mansion in the Federal style. Successive Presidents and their wives have redecorated and restored the mansion to their own taste – most notably Jacqueline Kennedy from 1961 to 1963, when she re-discovered many nineteenth century furnishings that had been stored out of sight for decades. Ten years later Patricia Nixon supervised the re-decoration of the public rooms.

The President works in the Oval Office on the ground floor, surrounded by his closest advisers. The family living quarters are on the floor above. Among the facilities for relaxation are a cinema, bowling alley and swimming pool. Many Presidents have adopted the habit of hosting concerts or recitals by leading artists for important visitors. The state and public rooms at the White House are open to the public for free guided tours on most days throughout the year. Some 30,000 people visit it every week. The queue for admission always looks daunting but it moves quickly.

In and out of office

The President has a second official home at Camp David, a mountain retreat in Maryland, a short helicopter hop from the White House. Most have liked to spend weekends there. He receives a salary of $200,000 plus $50,000 for expenses, plus a further $100,000 tax free to spend on travel and $20,000 on official entertainment. He has use of the presidential aircraft, Air Force One, and round-the-clock security – although that is more a burden than a perk of office. He travels abroad less often than other heads of government. Generally people prefer to go to Washington to see him.

The last thing a new President is thinking about when he enters the White House is what will happen to him when he leaves it. Yet that day will come and when it does his income will drop sharply. He will receive a pension of $80,000 plus an office, secretarial help and free postal facilities. He retains custody of his presidential papers. Modern Presidents customarily use the papers as the basis of a book about the administration, before presenting them to (or establishing) a library for their preservation.

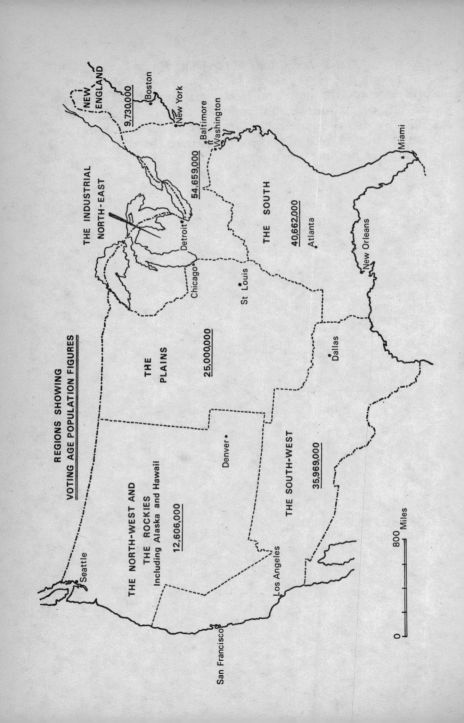

REGIONS SHOWING
VOTING AGE POPULATION FIGURES

NEW ENGLAND
9,730,000

THE INDUSTRIAL
NORTH-EAST
54,659,000

THE SOUTH
40,662,000

THE PLAINS
25,000,000

THE NORTH-WEST AND
THE ROCKIES
Including Alaska and Hawaii
12,606,000

THE SOUTH-WEST
35,969,000

Boston
New York
Baltimore
Washington
Miami
Detroit
Chicago
St Louis
Atlanta
New Orleans
Dallas
Denver
Seattle
San Francisco
Los Angeles

0   800 Miles

4

The Political Map

The United States is a deceptive country for those who know it only superficially, from a brief visit or as a background to films and television series. The first, false impression is one of unusual homogeneity: the shopping mall at Boston, Massachusetts, is as indistinguishable from the one at Albuquerque, New Mexico, as are their hotels and airports. The Howard Johnson's restaurants on the New Jersey Turnpike are no different from those on the Pacific Highway in California. The rich Texans in *Dallas* are hard to tell from the rich Denver folk in *Dynasty*.

Yet these familiar landmarks and stereotypes mask an immense regional and social diversity in terms of geography, economics, race, religion, attitudes and assumptions. New Americans, arriving from all over the world, have in general preferred to live among those of their own original nationality and to maintain the customs of their own native lands. A candidate for national office must endeavour to pitch an appeal across all such divisions.

In crude terms, that is why you will see him being photographed nibbling Jewish blintzes in Florida at breakfast time, southern hush puppies in Alabama for lunch and Polish sausages in Chicago for supper. The primary election trail is littered with the political corpses of men who have failed, at anything more than that symbolic level, to take account of the sensibilities of one or other of the important ethnic and regional minorities.

The fifty states of the USA have an area of 3,618,770 square miles. The Department of Commerce conducts a national census at the end of every decade. In 1980 the population was

found to be 226,545,805, although some critics said it had
been under-counted. It represented an increase of 11.4 per
cent over the 1970 figure. As the time for the 1990 census
draws near, the true head count is probably above 250
million.

In some respects the United States follows the pattern of
other industrialised countries, in that liberal and progressive
politicians do well in urban areas and among poorer manual
workers, while conservatives get their support from the
wealthy and the rural middle class. The Democratic Party is
dominant among trade unionists. It has traditionally been
regarded as more progressive than the Republican in that it
has favoured a higher level of public spending and of government involvement in the economy. Country and suburban
dwellers resent their taxes being devoted to relieving hardship
in the cities and consequently support the Republican policy
of low taxation (see page 145).

Franklin Roosevelt's New Deal in the 1930s had a similar
effect on American political attitudes to that of the 1940s
Labour Government in Britain. Never since has there been
significant mainstream opposition to providing at least
minimal welfare benefits for the most needy. Since
Roosevelt, more Americans have customarily registered as
Democrats than Republicans. Throughout the Reagan presidency, for instance, successive Gallup polls have found
around forty per cent of people declaring themselves to
be Democrats as against a Republican score of between thirty
and thirty-five per cent. But that has not deterred the
electorate from choosing Republican presidents in the last
four elections out of five, or from frequently plumping for
Republican congressmen and governors.

In any event, the distinction between the two parties is not
clear cut. There are as wide differences of philosophy within
as between them. Both are coalitions of interest groups. In
the 1970s, for instance, a large section of the white working
class, concerned about the growing number of non-whites
moving into the cities and irritated by 'liberal' student demonstrations, became more conservative. There were 'hard-hat'

marches in favour of the Vietnam war. Many who took part continued to count themselves as Democrats.

Again, until recently Democrats could always be assured of a majority amongst white voters in the south, both urban and rural. This dated from the Civil War and the south's hostility to the party of Abraham Lincoln. Southern Democrats were usually more conservative than the party's followers elsewhere but they were authentic Democrats nonetheless. Their loyalty to the official party began to break down in 1948, when the southern states voted for the 'Dixiecrat' Strom Thurmond instead of for Harry Truman. In 1964 the only states that voted for the Republican Barry Goldwater (with the exception of his political base in Arizona) were in the south. Today the Democratic candidate can no longer rely on southern support. In 1984 Ronald Reagan won sixty per cent or more of the vote in most southern states and even in 1980 Jimmy Carter won only one state in the region, his native Georgia. Of the eleven southern states listed in section 3 below, six have a Democratic governor and five a Republican. (See tables pages 194 to 195.) Most black people vote Democrat in all parts of the country.

Because of its diversity, America is best understood by dividing it into sections. There are many possible criteria for doing this. I have chosen a fairly conventional division into six reasonably cohesive regions. The tables below each section show how the states in the region voted in the last three presidential elections, together with the number of votes each commands in the electoral college. The change in the number of college delegates between the 1980 and 1984 elections reflects the new population figures in the most recent (1980) census. If the figure went down in 1984 it meant the state was losing population; if it increased it was gaining population. (See map on page 122.) In the tables, the candidate named first is the Republican. The figures do not add up to 100 per cent because of the intervention of third-party candidates.

1. New England

States: Connecticut, Maine, Massachusetts, New Hampshire, Rhode Island, Vermont. Voting-age population: 9,730,000

Chiefly Republican except for Boston, the only major city in the region. Only a small minority of the inhabitants can now trace their descent from the Pilgrims and the other early settlers in the seventeenth and eighteenth centuries, who made their first homes here, but the 'proper Bostonian' culture still survives among the few. With its large population of Irish descent, as well as its share of blacks and Hispanics, the city, the home of the Kennedys, has long been a Democratic stronghold. Democrats also gain support among staff and students at the academic institutions for which this region is noted. Two of the country's leading colleges are here – Harvard at Cambridge, near Boston, and Yale at New Haven, Connecticut.

The area was one of the earliest manufacturing centres in the United States, specialising in textiles and light engineering. By the 1970s most of that business had been lost, partly to the Far East, with its lower labour costs, and partly to the booming sunbelt of the southern and western United States. As factories were abandoned and decayed, the region, together with the north-east industrial states (see below) became known dismissively as the 'rustbelt'. Grandiose city centres, built in the optimistic days of the turn of the century, crumbled as a result of falling prosperity and the middle-class preference for living in the suburbs. Boston was one of the cities hit by disturbances in the 'long, hot summers' of the early 1960s, while the college campuses saw frequent demonstrations against the Vietnam war.

In the 1980s, however, there has been a revival in the region. Partly because of its proximity to academic institutions, this has become a centre for the new computer-based high-technology enterprises. The outskirts of Boston are packed with modern factories making advanced business equipment and precision machine tools, as well as medical equipment and supplies. The city itself has responded to this development by becoming a banking centre for people putting their money into new industries with a high risk factor. It is not the kind of finance that would have been associated with proper Boston at the turn of the century, but Americans are nothing if not adaptable.

The region's long-term population decline, dating from before World War Two, appears to be halting as a result of these changes, and unemployment is low. But because its new industries primarily serve a business market, New England would be especially vulnerable to a severe recession. The economic difficulties of Reagan's last years might test the loyalty of people who voted Republican last time.

HOW THEY VOTED

Number of electoral college votes in brackets.
Voting figures as %.)

	1976		1980		1984	
	Ford	Carter	Reagan	Carter	Reagan	Mondale
Connecticut	(8) 52.1	46.9	(8) 48.2	38.5	(8) 60.7	38.8
Maine	(4) 48.9	48.1	(4) 45.6	42.3	(4) 60.8	38.8
Massachusetts	(14) 40.4	56.1	(14) 41.9	41.7	(13) 51.2	48.4
New Hampshire	(4) 54.7	43.5	(4) 57.7	28.4	(4) 68.6	30.9
Rhode Island	(4) 44.1	55.4	(4) 37.2	47.7	(4) 51.8	47.9
Vermont	(3) 54.4	43.1	(3) 44.4	38.4	(4) 57.9	40.8

2. *The Industrial North-east*

States: Delaware, Indiana, Maryland, Michigan, New Jersey, New York, Ohio, Pennsylvania, Wisconsin. District of Columbia. Voting-age population: 54,659,000.

The decline of the heavy industries in this region, notably steel in Pittsburgh and motor car manufacture in Detroit, took longer to make itself felt than the comparable collapse of light industries in New England, and recovery has consequently been slower. Although this is still the most crowded region of the country there is a continuing shift of population towards the sunbelt states.

The big cities here – notably New York, Philadelphia, Cleveland and Baltimore – were for years the power base of the old-style Democratic Party machines run by all-powerful bosses who exercised control over patronage jobs and could be relied upon to bring out the votes at election time. The cities' Jewish, Irish, Italian and black communities have traditionally supported the Democrats, who remain the dominant urban party; but patronage jobs are fewer and the machines scarcely exist in their old forms. The children and grandchildren of the immigrants have prospered in business and the professions and have aspired to move away from the over-crowded city centres. In doing so they have also thrown off rigid party loyalties.

As people and businesses leave, many city centres – in some cases after years of decay – are being developed as tourist and leisure complexes with shopping malls and the like. Historic buildings have been restored as museums, craft shops, restaurants and in some cases expensive apartments. Skyscraper complexes of shops and offices are going up: one of the first was the Renaissance Centre in Detroit. In former major ports, such as New York and Baltimore, disused piers are being converted to similar purposes.

Tourism and the convention business are being developed to fill the void left by the departing industries. Attempts are being made to introduce the kind of high-tech enterprises that New England and the west coast have been able to attract. Banking and financial services are growing, especially in New York, but these are vulnerable to unfavourable economic conditions.

In most of these states, conservative voters in the suburbs and rural areas broadly balance the liberals of the cities, although New Jersey, with no really big cities and with a suburban overflow from Manhattan, tends more than neighbouring states to favour the Republicans. On the other hand the District of Columbia, all city with no hinterland, has voted overwhelmingly for the Democratic candidate since it was first allowed its three electoral college votes in 1964.

HOW THEY VOTED

(Number of electoral college votes in brackets.
Voting figures as %.)

| | 1976 | | 1980 | | 1984 | |
	Ford	Carter	Reagan	Carter	Reagan	Mondale
Delaware	(3) 46.6	52.0	(3) 47.2	44.8	(3) 59.8	39.9
D.C.	(3) 16.5	81.6	(3) 13.4	74.8	(3) 13.7	85.4
Indiana	(13) 53.3	45.7	(13) 56.0	37.7	(12) 61.7	37.7
Maryland	(10) 46.7	52.8	(10) 44.2	47.1	(10) 52.5	47.0
Michigan	(21) 51.8	46.4	(21) 49.0	42.5	(20) 59.2	40.2
New Jersey	(17) 50.1	47.9	(17) 52.0	38.6	(16) 60.1	39.2
New York	(41) 47.5	51.9	(41) 46.7	44.0	(36) 53.8	45.8
Ohio	(25) 48.7	48.9	(25) 51.5	40.9	(23) 58.9	40.1
Pennsylvania	(27) 47.7	50.4	(27) 49.6	42.5	(25) 53.3	46.0
Wisconsin	(11) 47.8	49.4	(11) 47.9	43.2	(11) 54.3	45.1

3. The South

States: Alabama, Florida, Georgia, Kentucky, Louisiana, Mississippi, North Carolina, South Carolina, Tennessee, Virginia, West Virginia. Voting-age population: 40,662,000

The fast-growing 'new south' has seen an impressive increase in population in the last thirty years. Industries and corporate offices have moved from the frosty north to this friendlier climate. As Edmund Fawcett and Tony Thomas point out in their book *America, Americans*, the single invention that made the rise of the south possible was air-conditioning. 'It is difficult to imagine economic takeoff in the old Confederacy, cooled only by ceiling fans.'

The skylines of major southern cities have become junior versions of Manhattan or Chicago, with modern glass skyscrapers soaring above what used to be main streets lined with low-rise buildings in the elegant southern colonial style. The

1980 census showed that the population of the south had grown by twenty-one per cent, compared with a national rate of eleven per cent.

The old caricature of the sleepy, rural south had it peopled by slow-talking, deeply conservative straw-chewers, who practised rigid discrimination against the large black population (eighteen per cent of the total). Today that image comes nowhere close to reality. The new southerner is likely to be a high-pressure executive flying across the nation drumming up business for his company and his region. Atlanta airport is the country's second busiest.

The rise of the new south is not simply a matter of the weather: many firms have been attracted by the fact that the trade unions have nowhere near as strong a hold here as in the north. An exception is in the Appalachian coalfields in the north of the region: Kentucky, West Virginia and Tennessee. But even here union power has declined as national demand for coal has decreased and an increasing proportion of it is being mined by open-cast methods in central and western states, where the unions are weak.

Despite rapid changes, some of the region's former character remains. Kentucky and Tennessee are still the centres of the Bourbon whiskey industry – one of the few that is still conducted largely along traditional lines – although consumption of hard liquor in America has declined as wine has grown in popularity. Politically, many of the country's most conservative figures – from both parties – still come from the south. The social system is more stable here than elsewhere and many descendants of the old white southern families have stayed put. Class distinctions are still evident and public manners and morals quite formal.

Although race relations have improved dramatically, the prevailing ethos among white southerners is still to the right of that in other parts of the country. The south, the old 'bible belt', is also the headquarters of many of the fundamentalist evangelical churches that have gained millions of followers through their television broadcasts and whose political influence is conservative (see Pat Robertson, page 159). Moral issues such as abortion play a significant role in people's voting decisions here.

Florida has a special character because its near-tropical climate attracts elderly people who can afford to retire here. They generally lift the Republican vote tally above that in other southern states despite the aberration of Miami, on the state's southern tip. This is a unique city, predominantly Hispanic, a centre of the US drugs traffic and of other commerce with Latin America, and home to a sizeable contingent of refugees from Fidel Castro's Cuba. Its growth in the 1970s was partly responsible for the sharp increase in Florida's congressional representation after the 1980 census (see table below).

HOW THEY VOTED

(Number of electoral college votes in brackets.
Voting figures at %.)

	1976		1980		1984	
	Ford	Carter	Reagan	Carter	Reagan	Mondale
Alabama	(9) 42.6	55.7	(9) 48.8	47.5	(9) 60.5	38.3
Florida	(17) 46.6	51.9	(17) 55.5	38.5	(21) 65.3	34.7
Georgia	(12) 33.0	66.7	(12) 41.0	55.8	(12) 60.2	39.8
Kentucky	(9) 45.6	52.8	(9) 49.1	47.6	(9) 60.0	39.4
Louisiana	(10) 46.0	51.7	(10) 51.2	45.7	(10) 60.8	38.2
Mississippi	(7) 47.7	49.6	(7) 49.4	48.1	(7) 61.9	37.4
North Carolina	(13) 44.2	55.2	(13) 49.3	47.2	(13) 61.9	37.9
South Carolina	(8) 43.1	56.2	(8) 49.4	48.1	(8) 63.6	35.6
Tennessee	(10) 42.9	55.9	(10) 48.7	48.4	(11) 57.8	41.6
Virginia	(12) 49.3	48.0	(12) 53.0	40.3	(12) 62.3	37.1
West Virginia	(6) 41.9	58.0	(6) 45.3	49.8	(6) 54.7	44.3

4. The South-west

States: Arizona, California, New Mexico, Texas. Voting-age population: 35,969,000

Illegal immigrants from Mexico pour across the sparsely policed southern borders of California and Texas, usually by night and usually on foot. Many are caught and sent home but that does not deter them from trying again. They get work in the fields picking the fruit and vegetables that are among California's most important products. Their presence gives the south-western USA a Latin-American feel but does not directly affect its political character because they are not entitled to vote.

Los Angeles also attracts millions of Asian immigrants, legal and illegal. It is the centre of the entertainment industry – films and television – and the base for many weapons and aircraft manufacturers. The white population, too, has been expanding rapidly since before World War Two. Because of the mild climate, southern California, Arizona and New Mexico, like Florida, are popular with retired people. This helps produce a conservative political temper.

The northern part of the state is a contrast in terms of politics, climate and life-style. Where Los Angeles and the Mexican border lands are warm and arid, San Francisco and its surroundings are cool and damp. Where the south is characterised by surfers, beach bums and a predominantly sybaritic outlook, the north is more cerebral and earnest.

San Francisco, in appearance the most European city in the United States, is the financial centre of the western half of the country. It has also been the birthplace of some of the most influential political movements of the last thirty years. Early opposition to the Vietnam war was expressed on the University of California campus at Berkeley, whence it spread to other colleges. San Francisco was the birthplace of 'flower power' and the hippie cult of the 1960s, a movement based on a curious mixture of hedonism and ecology. It can lay claim to being America's most liberal city and for that reason has attracted a large and demonstrative population of homosexuals, who have become a significant force in local politics.

The nation's first and largest high-technology manufacturing area is just south of San Francisco in what has become known as Silicon Valley. Like its more recent counterpart in New England, it grew there because of the high quality research being undertaken in local academic institutions. The nearby Napa Valley is the centre of the United States wine industry, whose reputation has improved internationally in the last decade.

Texas – one of the fastest-growing states in the union – enjoys its image as a raucous, virile place whose larger-than-life inhabitants eat enormous red-blooded steaks, drink immoderately and enjoy themselves exuberantly. Like most stereotypes it is exaggerated, but it is true that there were never many peace demonstrators or flower children here. The Texas life-style is characterised by the rodeo, the wide-brimmed hat and the barbecue, symbols of the great outdoors and the state's cattle-ranching past.

Here, too, the political tenor is conservative; but not excessively so, for the state went to Hubert Humphrey in 1968 and Jimmy Carter in 1976. Houston and Dallas, its two largest cities, have downtown areas containing dramatic modern architecture. Houston is the centre of the US oil industry and its fortunes rise and fall with the oil price. It is also the headquarters of the national space programme, whose self-confidence was damaged by the accident to the shuttle in 1986. Dallas is now one of the most important business centres in the country.

Arizona is the home of Senator Barry Goldwater, the defeated Republican presidential candidate in 1964. As the figures on page 120 show, it is one of the most solidly Republican states in the west.

HOW THEY VOTED

(Number of electoral college votes in brackets.
Voting figures as %.)

	1976		1980		1984	
	Ford	Carter	Reagan	Carter	Reagan	Mondale
Arizona	(6) 56.4	39.8	(6) 60.6	28.2	(7) 60.5	38.3
California	(45) 49.3	47.6	(45) 52.7	35.9	(47) 57.5	41.3
New Mexico	(4) 50.5	48.1	(4) 54.9	36.7	(5) 54.9	36.7
Texas	(26) 48.0	51.1	(26) 55.3	41.4	(29) 63.6	36.1

5. *The North-west and the Rockies*

States: Alaska, Colorado, Hawaii, Idaho, Montana, Nevada, Oregon, Utah, Washington, Wyoming. Voting-age population: 12,606,000

The Rocky Mountains and the desert beneath make much of this area uncultivable and uninhabitable. It is, however, rich in energy resources. Some mining of coal and other minerals is undertaken in most of these states, especially Alaska and Wyoming. Extensive reserves are available for when the nation's other sources of supply begin to run out. There is also a certain amount of agriculture – Idaho is noted for its potatoes – and the mountain states are developing a year-round recreation industry. The ski resorts of Colorado thrive in winter while in summer there are ranches in Wyoming and Montana for open-air holidays. Alaska, separated from the rest of the United States by the equally empty expanses of western Canada, will never be a holiday resort but it contains one of the country's largest oil fields.

A recurring dilemma in all these states is deciding how much development can be allowed without destroying the wilderness character of the environment. Colorado, for instance, increased its population by nearly a third between the 1970 and 1980 censuses. Environmental pressure will become more acute if and when the time comes to exploit the region's energy resources more rapidly. Nearly all the coal in this area is extracted by open-cast methods that damage the landscape.

There are four large settlements: Denver, the capital of Colorado; Las Vegas, a frenetic gambling resort; Seattle, dominated by the Boeing aircraft company; and Portland, a large naval town. But these do not provide enough inner-city liberals to balance the rural conservatives. Utah, dominated by the Mormon church, gave Ronald Reagan a larger percentage of its vote than any other state in both 1984 and 1980, with Idaho not far behind.

Hawaii, a group of Pacific islands admitted as the 50th state in 1959, has thriving tourist and fruit-growing industries. Its voters incline toward the Democrats more than those of other states in this group.

HOW THEY VOTED

(Number of electoral college votes in brackets.
Voting figures as %.)

	1976		1980		1984	
	Ford	Carter	Reagan	Carter	Reagan	Mondale
Alaska	(3) 57.9	35.7	(3) 54.3	26.4	(3) 66.6	29.9
Colorado	(7) 54.0	42.6	(7) 55.1	31.1	(8) 63.4	35.1
Hawaii	(4) 48.1	50.6	(4) 42.9	44.8	(4) 55.1	43.8
Idaho	(4) 59.3	36.8	(4) 66.5	25.2	(4) 72.4	26.4
Montana	(4) 52.8	45.4	(4) 56.8	32.4	(4) 60.5	38.2
Nevada	(3) 50.2	45.8	(3) 62.5	26.9	(4) 65.8	32.0
Oregon	(6) 47.8	47.6	(6) 48.3	38.7	(7) 55.9	43.7
Utah	(4) 62.4	33.6	(4) 72.8	20.6	(5) 74.5	24.7
Washington	(9) 50.0	46.1	(9) 49.7	37.3	(10) 56.2	42.9
Wyoming	(3) 59.3	39.8	(3) 62.6	28.0	(3) 69.1	27.7

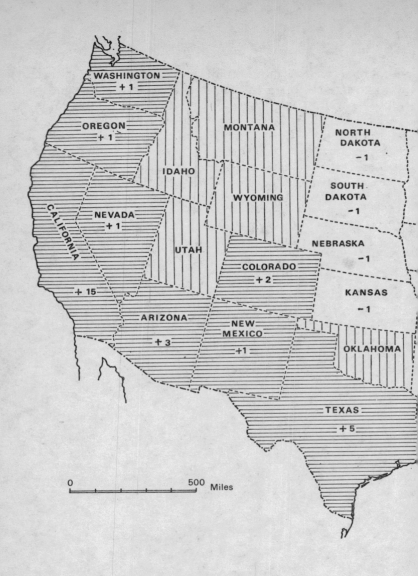

The drift to the Sun: the map shows the change in each State's representation in the electoral college between 1952 and 1988. Because representation is based on population, it is a measure of the move away from the industrial North-East and rural mid-West to the Sunbelt states of the South and West.

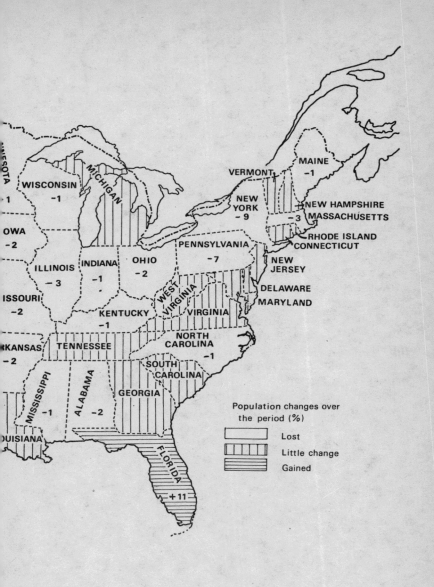

MAINE
−1

VERMONT

WISCONSIN
−1

MICHIGAN

NEW
YORK
−9

NEW HAMPSHIRE
−3 MASSACHUSETTS

RHODE ISLAND
CONNECTICUT

IOWA
−2

PENNSYLVANIA
−7

NEW
JERSEY

ILLINOIS
−3

INDIANA
−1

OHIO
−2

DELAWARE

MISSOURI
−2

WEST
VIRGINIA

VIRGINIA

MARYLAND

KENTUCKY
−1

ARKANSAS
−2

TENNESSEE

NORTH
CAROLINA
−1

SOUTH
CAROLINA

MISSISSIPPI
−1

ALABAMA
−2

GEORGIA

LOUISIANA

Population changes over
the period (%)

Lost

Little change

Gained

FLORIDA
+11

6. *The Plains*

States: Arkansas, Illinois, Iowa, Kansas, Minnesota, Missouri, Nebraska, North Dakota, Oklahoma, South Dakota. Voting-age population: 25,000,000

The plains states that make up the traditional farm belt have been badly hit by the fall in grain prices caused by over-supply. The result has been a slow decline in an already comparatively sparse population, with some small towns virtually abandoned, although not to the extent caused by the combined effects of depression and drought in the Dust Bowl era of the 1930s. At the 1928 election the total number of electoral college votes commanded by these states was 119. Today they can muster only 85. Many of the inhabitants are descendants of the northern Europeans, chiefly Germans and Scandinavians, who trekked west from the coast to settle here.

Chicago, where hundreds of thousands of East European immigrants settled, grew to importance as the mid-western market-place for cattle and farm produce. Today it is a commercial and banking centre, boasting the world's busiest airport. Apart from that city and the farms, the only major industry is defence: many of America's nuclear missiles are based in this area. A combination of the military presence and a predominantly rural population means that the Republicans do well in most of these states, although Minnesota provided the only victory (apart from DC) in 1984 for Walter Mondale, whose home state it is. The bad time they have had during the Reagan administration could test voters' loyalty this year. The candidate who makes the most credible promises to farmers is likely to do best here.

HOW THEY VOTED

(Number of electoral college votes in brackets.
Voting figures as %.)

	1976		1980		1984	
	Ford	Carter	Reagan	Carter	Reagan	Mondale
Arkansas	(6) 34.9	64.5	(6) 48.1	47.5	(6) 60.5	38.3
Illinois	(26) 50.1	48.1	(26) 49.6	41.7	(24) 56.2	43.3
Iowa	(8) 49.5	48.5	(8) 51.3	38.6	(8) 53.3	45.9
Kansas	(7) 52.5	44.9	(7) 57.9	33.3	(7) 66.3	32.6
Minnesota	(10) 42.0	54.9	(10) 42.6	46.5	(10) 49.5	49.7
Missouri	(12) 47.5	51.1	(12) 51.2	44.3	(11) 60.0	40.0
Nebraska	(5) 59.2	38.5	(5) 65.9	26.0	(5) 70.6	28.8
North Dakota	(3) 51.6	45.8	(3) 64.2	26.3	(3) 64.8	33.8
Oklahoma	(8) 50.0	48.7	(8) 60.5	35.0	(8) 68.6	30.7
South Dakota	(4) 50.4	48.9	(4) 60.5	31.7	(3) 63.0	36.5

5

The Political System

The United States Constitution lays down the framework of a system of federal government based on three separate and mutually restraining sets of powers: legislative, executive and judicial, in that order. The Constitution may be amended and has been from time to time. Amendments may be initiated by a two-thirds majority vote of both chambers of Congress, or through a constitutional convention called for by at least two-thirds of the original state governments. In either case, they have to be ratified by three-quarters of the state legislatures before they come into effect.

The details of the federal system – including its relation to the individual state legislatures – have thus been refined over the years, both by amendments and by interpretative decisions of the Supreme Court; but the framework remains intact and is the foundation of American democracy.

1. The Legislative Branch

Legislative powers are exercised by a two-chamber Congress comprising the Senate and the House of Representatives.

THE SENATE, the upper house, is made up of two senators from each of the fifty states of the union, regardless of their population. Members serve a six-year term. A third of them come up for election in November every two years, in the same years as elections for the House of Representatives. The elections are held on a statewide basis. Senators must be at least thirty years old, must have been US citizens for at least nine years and must be resident in the state that elects them. They are paid $75,100 per year. The Vice-President takes the chair at meetings of the Senate and has the casting vote in the event of a tie – one of the few constitutional functions he has.

THE HOUSE OF REPRESENTATIVES, the lower house, has 435 members, elected by congressional districts whose boundaries are drawn so that each should represent approximately half a million constituents. The Constitution originally stated that there should be one member for every 30,000 Americans but with a fast-growing population that requirement was clearly impossible to sustain, and the number of representatives is now fixed at 435. They are elected every two years – a shorter term than in most other democracies, meaning that they have their eyes almost permanently on the next election. This makes them especially sensitive to local feelings on contentious issues – as it is supposed to. It is part of the reason for the incidence of what is known as 'pork barrel politics' (see below, page 130).

Representatives must be at least twenty-five years old, citizens of at least seven years' standing and residents of the state they represent. They are paid $75,100 a year, the same as senators. As its presiding officer, the House of Representatives elects a Speaker from among members of the majority party. He receives $97,900 a year plus expenses.

Before the 1988 election the Democrats held majorities in both houses – by fifty-four to forty-six in the Senate and 257 to 178 in the House, where the District of Columbia, Guam, American Samoa and the Virgin Islands are each allowed one non-voting representative. (See table page 194.) Both chambers are unrepresentative in terms of race and sex. The Senate, which over the years has managed to retain the atmosphere of a white men's club, has no black members and only two women, one from each party. The lack of blacks is partly explained by the fact that senate elections are on a statewide basis and no state has more than thirty-five per cent of blacks (Mississippi). The current House of Representatives has twenty-three black people – all Democrats – and twenty-four women, thirteen Democrats and eleven Republicans. Nationally, the black proportion of the population is twelve per cent.

The congressional session begins on 3 January each year and ends when members decide to adjourn, although the President can call them back to a special session to discuss legislation he particularly wants to see enacted. The two bodies meet in separate chambers in the Capitol building on Capitol Hill in Washington. Their meetings are open to the public.

The powers of Congress are stated in great detail in the Constitution. The main ones are:

    To levy taxes and collect them;
    To raise loans for the public purse;
    To regulate trade with foreign countries, and between the
        states of the union;
    To make laws for naturalisation of foreign citizens;
    To coin money, decide its value, fix an exchange rate with
        overseas currencies, fix punishments for counterfeiters
        and set standards for weights and measures;
    To establish post offices;
    To legislate patent and copyright laws;
    To establish a federal court system;
    To declare war and punish piracy;
    To raise and support an army and a navy, make rules for
        running them and to call the militia into action against
        foreign and domestic threats;
    To make laws for the District of Columbia; and
    To make all laws necessary to execute the above powers
        and others that derive from the Constitution.

The power to declare war is perhaps the most significant of all. It puts a brake on the conduct of foreign policy by the President and the executive branch. Presidents have often sought to circumvent this restriction and sometimes succeeded (e.g. President Johnson and the Tonkin Gulf resolution – see page 55). But ultimately the power remains as an important check to an overweening executive.

A rarely-used additional power with the same effect is to impeach public servants, including the President, for offences committed in office. The impeachment powers are split between the two chambers. The 'trial' is undertaken by the House of Representatives; but once the victim is found guilty, only the Senate can formally remove him from office.

As well as stating the powers of Congress, the Constitution expressly forbids certain acts. Congress may not:

Suspend the right of *habeas corpus*, except at times of rebellion or invasion or when the public safety requires it;

Pass laws allowing for conviction and condemnation without trial;

Pass laws retroactively;

Levy any direct taxes except on the basis of census returns;

Impose tariffs on exports from any state or allow preferential treatment to vessels using the ports of any one state;

Authorise any honours system, or allow federal officials to accept foreign honours without the permission of Congress.

Further restrictions on Congressional powers were imposed by ten constitutional amendments, known as the Bill of Rights, ratified in 1791. These are listed on page 136. The tenth of them limits the powers of Congress to those spelled out in the Constitution and declares that all other powers belong to state legislatures or to the people. This has been the basis of the frequent clashes between Washington and state legislatures over the right of states to control their own affairs, particularly in respect of the civil rights of their citizens.

Legislation within the above limits may be initiated in either chamber of Congress, except that revenue bills must have their origin in the House of Representatives; the Senate, though, has the same power to amend or ultimately reject such bills as it has over any others.

There are many ways in which legislation may be introduced. The President has the power to ask Congress to consider certain bills. Other members of the executive may also suggest bills on their own account, as can any member of Congress. Many bills are also initiated by the specialist standing committees in both houses – sixteen in the Senate and twenty-two in the House.

These committees are a vital part of the legislative process. They are chaired by a member of the majority party and their membership is proportional to party representation in the relevant chamber. All legislation, however introduced, is sent to the committee concerned in the Senate or House of Representatives, whichever originated it. For instance, a bill concerning farms, introduced in the Senate, would go to the Senate agriculture committee.

The committee usually holds public hearings on the proposals, at which interested parties are invited to express their views. The committee will then propose amendments, often in response to representations made to it, and send the bill back to the full House or Senate, where it is debated by all the members. If approved, it is sent to the other chamber, which can either pass it unamended or suggest its own amendments. In the latter case it goes before a conference committee including members from both chambers, to arrive at a form of wording acceptable to both.

Voting seldom follows strict party lines in either chamber; and even less often is it a question of conscience. Often a member's vote is the subject of deals with the administration or with other members on the principle known as 'pork barrel politics'. To bolster their popularity with their constituents, members persuade the federal government to provide funds for local projects. This in turn can be achieved by 'log rolling', where the member will trade his support on administration measures for commitments to such expenditure. Alternatively, members may bargain between themselves for support on each other's projects or on bills in which their constituents have a particular interest. Such deals cut across party lines and help explain why members of Congress do not automatically vote the party ticket, as happens in most other legislative systems. On important matters, the administration may have to negotiate separately with nearly every Congress member for support. One example was the passage of the Panama Canal treaty ratification under President Carter (see page 67).

Once passed in identical form by both chambers, a bill goes to the President for his signature. If he agrees, it becomes law. He has the right, however, to veto it, in which case his veto can be over-ridden only by a two-thirds majority in both chambers. A third option for the President is to follow neither of those courses, in which case the bill automatically becomes law, without his signature, ten days after it was sent to him, unless Congress has adjourned by then.

Congress has an additional power that has come into particular prominence in recent years. It can establish committees to conduct public investigations in a number of areas, notably into the acts of officials. This was how the public came to know the details of the Watergate scandal under President Nixon and of the Iran/Contra affair under President Reagan. People who refuse to give evidence before these committees when asked may be cited for contempt of Congress – a device used at the McCarthy hearings into alleged communist influence in the administration in the 1950s (see page 45).

2. The Executive Branch

The President is the chief executive. He is also the commander-in-chief of the armed forces and the head of state. His powers are described in full in Chapter 1; his term and conditions of office, and the method used to elect him, in Chapter 3.

The executive branch over which he presides includes thirteen departments run by members of his Cabinet, plus more than 100 independent agencies. It disposes of a federal budget of close to $1,000 billion a year. Some three million civilians and two million servicemen are employed in and by it. The thirteen departments are listed below in the order in which they were established. Each is headed by a Cabinet member known as 'Secretary of . . .' followed by the name of the department, with the exception of the Justice Department, headed by the Attorney General. Members of the Cabinet are paid $81,000 a year. They may not be members of Congress. The departments are:

State: One of the two Cabinet offices that date from the first presidency, its original functions spanned domestic as well as foreign affairs. Today it deals only with relations with other countries. It supervises the foreign service; negotiates treaties; advises on the recognition of foreign governments; issues passports to US citizens and visas to overseas visitors; administers non-military aid to developing countries.

Treasury: The other original Cabinet office. It collects taxes; supervises the currency and the printing of postage stamps; pays government debts; operates the Secret Service; operates the Customs Service and regulates the sale of liquor between states.

Defense: Created in 1947 with the merger of the separate departments for the army, navy and air force. Controls a budget of $282,150 million a year, more than a quarter of all federal expenditure.

Justice: The Attorney General, as the chief law officer, oversees all government legal action, supervising district attorneys throughout the country. The department includes the Federal Bureau of Investigation (FBI), which looks into breaches of federal rather than state laws. The Immigration and Naturalisation Service also comes under the Justice Department.

Interior: Charged with protecting the environment and developing the natural resources of the land. It runs national parks, monuments and historic sites, regulates hunting and fishing and oversees the running of reservations for American Indians.

Agriculture: Assists farmers and regulates prices and markets. Researches improved methods of agriculture.

Commerce: Oversees business; regulates weights and measures; issues weather forecasts; publishes nautical charts; conducts census every ten years.

Labor: Provides employment statistics; regulates health, safety, working hours and conditions; provides training schemes.

Health and Human Services: Created as the Department of Health, Education and Welfare in 1953, when it became clear that in a modern society these functions could not be left wholly in the hands of the state governments. (President Carter created a separate Department of Education in 1979.) Runs the social security services, including free medical care for elderly people. Social security cost $207,504 million in 1987, the second highest item on the national budget after defence. Operates the Food and Drug Administration and the Center for Disease Control.

Housing and Urban Development: Co-ordinates urban renewal and development in public and private sectors. Created in 1965 when, like health and welfare, housing was becoming more and more a concern of central government as well as of the states.

Transportation: Supervises road construction and vehicle regulations; controls civil aviation (through the Federal Aviation Administration). Also responsible for rail, sea and river travel, and for the Coast Guard.

Energy: Created in 1977 in response to the energy crisis, to look into ways of exploiting and increasing the country's energy resources.

Education: Hived off from Health and Human Resources in 1979 (see above). Administers federal aid to education. Running ordinary schools is the responsibility of local authorities.

Since 1939 the President has, in addition, had his own executive office, including his personal White House staff of advisers, who over the years have grown in numbers and come to play an ever larger role in formulating policy. When Harry

Truman succeeded to the presidency in 1945 the staff of the Executive Office of the President numbered around fifty. By the end of his term it was up to 250 and when President Kennedy took over eight years later it was close to 3,000. Today it is more than 5,000.

Tension and rivalries have grown up between White House staff and Cabinet members as to which has the right to exercise the greater influence over the President. Appointments to both sets of positions are in the gift of the President but, because he has more day-to-day contact with the White House staff by virtue of their physical proximity, they have usually come out on top. To some extent, however, the pecking order is decided by the personal qualities of the men and women involved.

The National Security Adviser, at the head of the National Security Council, has attracted the most attention among White House staffers, ever since McGeorge Bundy was appointed to the post by President Kennedy in 1961 and carved out a wide area of power for himself. The council itself was created in 1947. Henry Kissinger was the best known National Security Adviser, eclipsing the Secretary of State as the strongest foreign policy voice in the Nixon administration until he took over at the State Department himself.

The power of the National Security Council under President Reagan was demonstrated by the revelations about its role in arranging arms supplies to Iran in an attempt to obtain the release of US hostages in Lebanon. This was done against the wishes and advice of the two Cabinet members most concerned – the Secretary of State, George Shultz, and the Secretary of Defense, Caspar Weinberger, who resigned not long after the congressional hearings on the issue in 1987.

The Office of Management and Budget, also inside the White House, often plays a greater role in formulating fiscal policy than the Treasury Department. Formerly called the Budget Bureau, it was given new powers and a new name by President Nixon in 1970. At the same time he established a Domestic Council under John Ehrlichman, with the idea that he should exercise the same authority on the home front as

Kissinger did over foreign affairs. In this way he was trying to centralise power in the White House and override members of his Cabinet whom he believed – as heads of government customarily do believe – to be too much dominated by the senior civil servants in their departments. This experiment was quickly submerged, like so much else in Washington, by the Watergate scandal, which claimed Ehrlichman as an early victim. Whether it would have succeeded otherwise is unknowable.

3. The Judicial Branch

The United States has a unique twin-track system of state and federal courts that exercise jurisdiction in separate (though sometimes overlapping) areas. It was the result of a compromise at the Constitutional Convention, where some delegates did not want a federal court system at all, believing that the states should have sovereignty over all legal affairs. The finally agreed version of the Constitution provides the basis of the country's legal system:

> The judicial power of the United States shall be vested in one Supreme Court and such inferior courts as the Congress may from time to time ordain and establish.

Essentially the federal courts hear cases arising from federal rather than state laws and offences that have occurred in more than one state. Although there are no formal checkpoints on state boundaries, federal offences are committed by transporting certain items between states (e.g. liquor or women intending to engage in prostitution). An offence is also committed by sending fraudulent material through the US mails. Such laws give the federal courts legislation in cases involving, for instance, large-scale organised crime, and allow the FBI to investigate them.

Below the Supreme Court are eleven appeal courts and ninety-one district courts, plus three special courts to deal with financial claims against the government, military appeals and customs matters and patents. Judges are appointed by Congress and may not be dismissed except in cases of blatant misbehaviour, when they can be impeached like other federal officers. Although their initial appointment is often made on political grounds, their security of tenure gives the judges a wide measure of independence from the legislature.

The framework of the American legal system is the so-called Bill of Rights, ten amendments to the Constitution ratified in 1791. These prevent Congress from restricting citizens' rights to:

> Freedom of speech, religion, peaceful assembly and the right to petition for redress of grievances;
> Keep and bear arms;
> Refuse to have soldiers billeted on him;
> Be secure against search without warrant;
> Not be tried without indictment before a grand jury; nor be tried twice for the same offence; nor give self-incriminatory evidence; nor be deprived of life, liberty or property without due process of law; nor forfeit his property for public use without compensation; (this is the Fifth Amendment.)
> A speedy trial;
> Trial by jury in civil cases;
> No excessive bail requirement;
> Limit Congress to the powers delegated to it by the Constitution: other powers belong to the state legislatures or the people.

THE SUPREME COURT consists of a chief justice and eight associate justices. At least six of the judges must be present before the court can sit. Their decisions do not have to be unanimous. It is the final court of appeal for the federal court system but its most significant role is to interpret the Constitution and decide whether certain acts of the federal and state governments are in breach of it. Its right to be the final arbiter in such cases was affirmed by Chief Justice John Marshall in a ringing judgment in the landmark case of Marbury *v.* Madison in 1803. He declared:

> The Constitution is either a superior paramount law, unchangeable by ordinary means, or it is on a level with ordinary legislative acts and, like other acts, is alterable when the legislature shall please to alter it. If the former part of the alternative be true, then a legislative act contrary to the Constitution is not law; if the latter part be true then constitutions are absurd attempts, on the part of the people, to limit a power in its own nature illimitable.

In deciding unambiguously in favour of the first of these alternatives, Marshall set out the historic principle that 'a legislative act contrary to the Constitution is not law', and added that 'it is emphatically the province and duty of the judicial department to say what the law is'. But even within that role of defining and enforcing the Constitution there is room for disagreement. Some justices are 'strict constructionists', which means that they interpret the Constitution literally as far as possible and do not believe that it should be reinterpreted to accord with changed circumstances. The opposite view is that the spirit of the Constitution is more important ·than the letter and that the Court's decisions should reflect that in cases where the intentions of the framers have clearly been overtaken by events.

Supreme Court justices are nominated by the President but their appointment has to be ratified by Congress. Presidents customarily nominate people who share their political views – and not always people with much judicial experience. This is less of an oddity than it might seem to those who believe in the concept of a non-political judiciary, since many of the decisions the court makes are inherently political, and the justices often divide along political lines.

Clashes from time to time occur when a President nominates someone to the Supreme Court whose political views and judicial record make him objectionable to a majority in Congress. This is especially liable to happen when Congress is not controlled by the President's party. Presidents Nixon and Reagan both lost battles with Congress to have their first choices (and in Reagan's case his second choice also) ratified.

Such cases always make headlines. To outsiders, they may seem to symbolise an anarchic element in the American system of government. In fact, they are the clearest possible manifestation of the checks and balances inherent in that system. The court's membership is decided by the President, with Congress able to exercise a veto. Once appointed, the judges have the power to rule on matters involving the authority of both the Congress and the President. In doing so, however, they have to abide by the Constitution, which Congress and the states have the power to amend. So none of the three branches of government is supreme.

State and local government

Most major functions other than those patently the responsibility of the federal administration – such as foreign affairs and defence – are controlled by the state governments. But that simple statement masks a whole series of 'grey' areas where power is exercised in tandem. As the nation has developed and its problems grown more complex, Washington has assumed greater responsibilities. As noted earlier in this chapter, health, education, welfare and housing were originally seen as matters for individual states until it was recognised that a national effort was required to ensure that help went to the people who needed it most. And on civil rights, the federal government and the Supreme Court found it necessary to goad some reluctant states into conforming with nationally accepted standards.

State legislatures are miniature versions of the federal government. As with Washington, the seat of government is not usually in the state's largest city: in New York state, for instance, it is at Albany and in California at Sacramento. State governments are split into the same three branches as federal: legislative, executive and judicial. All states have an elected governor to perform the executive role, with powers similar to those of the President but on a smaller canvas. Except in North Carolina, the governor has a veto power which can be overturned by a two-thirds majority of legislators. He can even call out the state contingent of the National Guard. The vice-presidential role at state level is usually taken by a lieutenant-governor, separately elected. A governor's 'cabinet', unlike a President's, is usually elected, not appointed – and so are judges in the state courts.

All states except Nebraska have an elected bicameral legislature, meeting in a building that in some cases greatly resembles the Capitol in Washington. (Nebraska has a single-chamber legislature.) Laws are passed on all matters relating to the state, with the proviso that they must not conflict with the federal Constitution. Procedures for introducing bills are based on those at national level.

Below the state governments are those of the cities, usually headed by a mayor. Their scale depends on the city's size but in large ones like New York and Chicago the mayor is an extremely influential and high-profile figure. Some small cities hire a professional city manager to run services on behalf of the council. Cities also have their own courts for minor cases, similar to magistrates' courts in Britain. Among the services run by city administrations are the police and fire brigade, street maintenance and cleaning, public hospitals, schools and libraries. Rural counties and towns have their own more modest local government system.

Elections for state offices are usually held on the same day as federal elections: the Tuesday after the first Monday in November. Some counties and cities also hold their elections on that day but in other cases – New York and Chicago are two – they are held at a different time of year.

All levels of government are financed by taxes. Every April Americans fill in separate returns for their federal (by far the largest), state and city income taxes. In addition, local administrations levy taxes on property and often a small sales tax on goods purchased there.

Sweeping the roads in a small town in North Dakota is at

Support for parties and President's approval rating
during Reagan's presidency

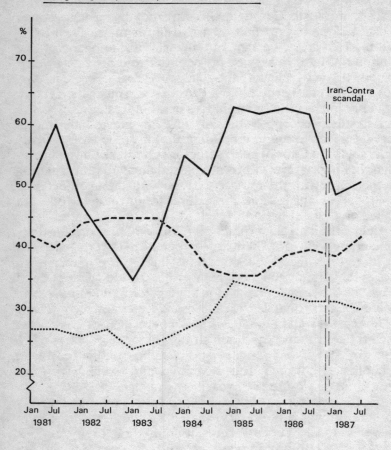

The President

The Democrats

The Republicans

Source — Gallup polls

the opposite end of the political spectrum from the decisions on war and peace reached at the White House. Yet the small-scale jobs have to be done efficiently and, under the American system, the people who run them are accountable to those they serve. They are part of the intricate pyramid of US democracy, at whose apex the President stands.

6

1988 – The Issues

Much reporting of the US election, especially in non-American newspapers and on television, concentrates on the personalities of the candidates rather than the political views dividing them. Yet their positions on the issues that most concern Americans play an important role in the campaign, not least in determining the level of funds they can raise. Donors will not give money to people they disagree with on matters of importance. (Big business, for instance, is unlikely to be enamoured of politicians who advocate higher corporate – or indeed personal – taxes.) Below is an outline of the main issues that confront the United States in 1988. In Chapter 7 the positions of the individual candidates on these issues are described in greater detail, and there is a table comparing their views on page 152.

The economy

President Reagan's most significant legacies to the nation are yawning trade and budget gaps, a weak dollar and a faltering stock market. Trouble had been brewing for some time but the extent of the crisis was not brought home to Americans until Black Monday, 19 October 1987, when the stock markets on Wall Street and around the world collapsed more dramatically than on any previous single day, even in 1929. Millions of people were plunged into varying degrees of financial crisis. At the end of a day when a record 600 million shares were traded, prices were 22.6 per cent lower than they had been the previous Friday, and more than $500 billion had been wiped off the paper value of securities.

Reagan's initial response was disconcertingly similar to statements made by the authorities in 1929, when the crash signalled the start of a long depression. 'The underlying economy remains sound,' he said. Not many experts agreed with him. They believed that the loss of business confidence was provoked by the chronic US trade and budget deficits, caused by soaring imports and by the President's philosophical abhorrence of tax increases. The projected trade deficit for 1987 was $170 billion and the budget deficit $148 billion – lower than the previous year but still unsustainable. America's foreign debt had reached $250 billion and some economists believed that left unchecked it would climb to $1,000 billion by 1992. The national debt – the amount owed by the federal government to internal and external lenders – was at $2,370 billion and interest payments amounted to nearly $150 billion, some fifteen per cent of the total budget outlay.

The budget deficit was also an important contributory factor to the trade gap. To finance the deficit the United States needed to attract foreign funds, which meant keeping interest rates high. The inrush of money pushed up the value of the dollar in world currency markets. This increased the price of American exports and made imports cheaper. So while Americans were buying cheaply from overseas, US manufacturers found their markets dwindling. In September 1985 the finance ministers of the five major western countries met in New York and agreed plans to force the value of the dollar down. This duly happened over the next three years but the trade gap remained: American consumers wanted foreign goods and were willing to pay the higher prices for them.

There are two ways of curing a budget deficit: to increase government revenue (i.e. taxes) or to reduce expenditure. To advocate higher personal or corporate taxes is a swift route to political oblivion, especially amongst Republicans. Bruce Babbitt, the ex-governor of Arizona, running for the Democratic nomination, was frankest of all the candidates in saying taxes would have to be raised, and he proposed a five per cent 'consumption tax', in effect a national sales tax. He received minimal support and was the first of the 'seven dwarfs' to pull

out of the race. It is also unpopular to propose cuts in areas of
spending that directly benefit important sections of the
populace, for instance welfare, farm price supports or road
building. Defence cuts go down badly with conservatives, and
of course with the defence industry.

Such pitfalls make it inadvisable for candidates to be too
specific about their economic programmes. They generalise
about the desirability of cutting expenditure and keeping
taxes low, while any precise proposals they make are about
the mechanics rather than the substance. In the primary
campaigns the three leading Republicans – George Bush,
Robert Dole and Jack Kemp – all advocated giving the
President 'line-item' veto power on budget measures, meaning that he could veto specific items in budget bills that he
thought profligate, without returning the whole bill to Congress. This has been a favourite proposal of past Presidents,
and Reagan, but it has never been agreed by Congress and is
unlikely to be, whoever becomes President in November.
This is because the most obvious targets for presidential cuts
would be the 'pork barrel' local spending programmes that
congressmen negotiate into the legislation to enhance their
re-election prospects in their constituencies. They would not
wish to forfeit that power. In any event, any savings made by
the use of such a device would make no significant dent in the
deficit.

The Democrats are less inhibited than the Republicans in
advocating drastic defence cuts: Jesse Jackson thinks spending in this area could be reduced by $20 billion without
seriously harming the nation's security. While none of the
other Democrats specified such a high figure, all agreed with
the principle. Many wanted to ditch the expensive new MX
missile system (recently renamed the Peacekeeper). Some
Democrats followed Babbitt in being prepared to recommend
a few limited tax increases, concentrating on high earners.
Some wanted to prevent purchasers of expensive houses from
claiming mortgage tax relief, others would tax social security
payments to the better off. Paul Simon advocated increasing
taxes on tobacco products.

Right-wing Republicans share President Reagan's philosophical doubt about whether tax increases really help reduce the budget deficit, as in theory they should. An important plank of his 1980 manifesto was the belief in the so-called 'Laffer curve', a mathematical model devised by Professor Arthur Laffer that sought to show that high taxes, by discouraging economic activity, actually reduce the amount of revenue flowing to the exchequer. Jack Kemp was one of the original apostles of this theory, which is why he presented himself in 1988 as the spiritual heir to Reagan, at least in the field of economic policy. But that did not appear to have helped his cause much.

Many candidates proposed raising federal revenue through a tax on imported oil, ranging from five to ten dollars a barrel. Higher import duties have the twin benefits of increasing revenues and protecting American industry, but the national philosophy has generally been opposed to protectionism. The idea of free trade accords well with the national spirit of self-reliance and, historically, with the national interest as well.

However, some candidates have been advocating retaliation in kind against countries that discriminate unfairly against American products. The Democrat Richard Gephardt had in fact sponsored legislation in Congress to that effect (see page 175) and stressed the issue in his primary campaigns. He drew a surprisingly enthusiastic reponse at first and many believed it was an important reason for his success in the early caucuses and primaries. Among the Republicans, only the evangelist Pat Robertson espoused a protectionist policy.

The trade deficit provoked a sharp fall in the value of the dollar in Reagan's last years. Between 1985 and the end of 1987, its value fell by fifty per cent against the world's other major currencies. This should have helped to correct the imbalance by making exports cheaper and imports (and foreign travel) dearer. There were signs that this was indeed happening. In January 1988, just before the first primaries, the deficit for November 1987 was announced: at $13.2

billion, it was an impressive twenty-five per cent lower than the figure for October – but still nothing like low enough to restore international confidence in the dollar. President Reagan remained unconvinced that drastic action was needed. 'The trade deficit could be a sign of economic strength,' he said at the beginning of 1988. His critics believed that his continued resistance to tax increases was storing up trouble for the next generation of Americans – and, more specifically, for the next President.

Welfare and education

There has always been a section of opinion on the American right which is opposed to welfare benefits of almost any kind, seeing them as un-American, conflicting with the national virtue of self-reliance. Only with Roosevelt's New Deal did any rudimentary welfare programme come into being, and it was strengthened by President Johnson's Great Society measures. Yet no candidate this year recommends any substantial cuts in the $325 billion annual welfare budget. To do so would alienate too many people who benefit from it – especially the elderly, who grow more and more significant as an electoral factor as life expectancy rises.

The average American now lives to seventy-five, compared with sixty-eight in 1950. Even right-wing Republican candidates proposed nothing more stringent in the way of welfare cuts than forcing the able-bodied to take any jobs available, on pain of forfeiting their benefits. Most also had plans to restrict the allocation of benefits to those who truly needed them, without getting into the specifics of how this could be accomplished. The 'welfare cheats' have long been an easy target for the right, but it is hard for them to campaign too vigorously on the issue, seeing that a right-wing President has been in office for the last eight years.

For the Democrats, Paul Simon advocated similar attempts at control, but most other Democratic candidates – notably Jesse Jackson – place the priority on increasing welfare benefits for the neediest. Candidates from both parties call for extra spending on AIDS research and some want mandatory testing for the disease, although this is opposed by liberals such as Jesse Jackson and Paul Simon.

Education is a perennial issue. Official figures say that twenty-three million adult Americans are illiterate. Parents are always dissatisfied with standards in the state schools and candidates habitually promise to improve them – although here too without spelling out how it can be done, short of massive extra expenditure. Higher pay for teachers was on the agenda of most of the Democrats, some of them linking the increase to merit. Right-wing Republicans favour an education voucher system, with every parent being given vouchers that can be exchanged at state or private schools. The most radical plan came from Pat Robertson, who called for the abolition of the Department of Education.

Moral issues

With two preachers among the candidates – Jesse Jackson and Pat Robertson – morals have loomed especially large this year. The single most contentious issue is a woman's right to choose abortion. Robertson is vociferously against it, saying that it threatens the values of the American family. The other right-winger, Jack Kemp, matched his ardour on the topic, while other Republicans were more circumspect: Bush, for instance, would allow abortions, but only in emergencies.

Robertson also drew a response in the American heartland with his denunciations of pornography, homosexuality and immorality in general, and his advocacy of compulsory daily prayer in schools. The moral constituency is a large one. In a poll in *Time* magazine in January 1988, a third of people questioned described themselves as born-again Christians – as President Carter was. If America is undergoing a moral revival, as those figures seem to indicate, Robertson seemed certain to be the beneficiary in electoral terms, no matter how hurriedly other Republicans tried to climb aboard the band wagon. Much-publicised sexual scandals involving two other television evangelists – Jim Bakker and Jimmy Swaggart – did not at first appear to harm his campaign, even though Swaggart had been an enthusiastic supporter of Robertson.

Jackson's moral appeal was of a different nature but none the less effective. He too spoke out against teenage pregnancies, but his approach was more sympathetic, less censorious than Robertson's. The reverse aspect of the moral issue was the fate of the Democrat Gary Hart, who found the electorate sternly unforgiving in the matter of his extra-marital relationship with Donna Rice, and languished at the bottom of the polls until he withdrew.

A moral issue with less impact on the electorate is corruption, or at least the hint of it. Several former members of the Reagan administration – and one surviving member, the Attorney General Edwin Meese – have been investigated on suspicion of taking part in dubious transactions involving pay-offs to third parties. One former White House aide, Michael Deaver, was convicted of perjury. The hearings into the Iran-Contra scandal (see page 71) revealed a morass of deception and double-dealing, including an attempt to trade arms sales for the release of hostages. But even though Vice-President Bush was clearly involved to some extent in Iran-Contra, it did not appear to harm his chances significantly.

Defence and East-West relations

The single issue that highlights the differences between the two parties on defence is the Strategic Defence Initiative (SDI, or Star Wars). President Reagan sets great store by this system which, when installed, would theoretically have the capability of destroying Soviet missiles aimed at American cities before they reached their targets. If the Americans had this system and the Russians did not, it would distort the balance of power between the two sides to such an extent that it would make nonsense of the theory of mutual deterrence and tension could increase to a perilous level. That, at least, is what the Russians and many American Democrats fear. The American/Soviet agreement to limit intermediate-range nuclear weapons (the INF agreement), eventually signed in Washington in December 1987, was delayed because the Russians initially wanted the Americans to give up Star Wars as part of the package.

All the Republican candidates were in favour of proceeding with Star Wars, despite its spiralling cost. The Democrats were split between those who oppose it totally (Dukakis, Gephardt and Simon) and those who would carry on researching the project with no commitment to deploying it (Gore and Jackson).

The INF agreement itself is opposed by conservative Republicans (represented by Kemp and Robertson) who distrust *rapprochement* with the Russians. They believe it is impossible to do deals with the communist leadership in the Soviet Union, which they regard as fundamentally evil and untrustworthy. For them the cold war is a natural and desirable state of affairs unless the Russians renounce communism. This is a populist view of long standing and Bush's enthusiastic endorsement of the deal thus did him no good on the right of his party, although he used it to solidify support in the centre by ensuring that he played a central role in Mr Gorbachev's visit for the signing of the treaty. He arranged to be photographed alongside the Soviet leader, underlining his role in the administration. Dole, with his eyes on the conservative wing of the party, was non-commital about the agreement for a while but later came down in its favour. The Democrats support it to a man.

Candidates from both parties – even those who favour *détente* – talk emotionally about keeping America strong and for that reason they are reluctant to advocate drastic reductions in defence spending. Only Jesse Jackson has unequivocal proposals for cutting back expenditure on weapons and switching the money to the welfare budget. But the clear economic need for savings deterred candidates from making commitments to spend more on defence – again with the exceptions of Kemp and Robertson. Candidates as disparate as Jackson and Dole exploited the old emotive issue of the amount America spends on keeping its 325,000 troops on the European mainland: they believe the Europeans should pay more for their own defence. Whoever the next President is, he is likely to want to make defence cuts soon after he takes office – and Europe seems the obvious place to start. Hart proposed the re-introduction of compulsory national service, but few supported that.

Contra aid and Irangate

The foreign policy issue closest to President Reagan's heart has been the provision of military and other help to the Contra rebels fighting the left-wing Sandinista government in Nicaragua. In 1979 the Sandinistas had overthrown the dictatorial President Anastasio Somoza, who had many friends on the American right. Nicaraguans who supported the former President (he was assassinated in exile in 1981) went to Honduras and began making military raids across the border into their home country.

Because the Sandinistas have friends in the communist world, American conservatives urged that it was in the strategic interest of the United States to support the rebels. But the Democratic majority in Congress was always reluctant to authorise military assistance, partly because they had doubts about supporting rebels bent on overthrowing a legitimate government by violent means, and partly because of the painful memories of Vietnam, which had brought home the perils of getting involved in other people's wars.

Americans have seldom played the role of world policeman with as much confidence as the British deployed in the nineteenth century. They are prepared to tolerate foreign wars only if it is crystal clear that a real national interest is at stake. There is no appetite for a crusade against communism unless it can be shown that the United States is directly threatened. The poorly resourced Sandinistas pose no credible challenge to a superpower, so there is little popular support in America for aiding their enemies.

It was the congressional opposition to Contra aid that provoked Reagan and his staff into trying to get help to the rebels clandestinely, using the proceeds of the secret arms sales to Iran. But even when the lid was blown off that ruse, Reagan did not end his efforts to provide help. At the end of 1987 he asked Congress to approve a package of civilian and military aid totalling $270 million. When it was clear that stood no chance of congressional approval, he scaled the request down to $36 million and undertook intensive lobbying of members. But he failed to swing enough votes his way. In his last year in office and discredited by the Iran/Contra affair, the President's power in Washington had dramatically waned. The House of Representatives rejected the aid proposal by a narrow 219 votes to 211.

In doing so it reflected the view of the people. According to opinion polls, seventy per cent of Democrats and fifty per cent of Republicans are against Contra aid. Despite that, all the Republican candidates spoke out in support of it. The charge of being 'soft on communism' remains a potent one in the party. The Democrats oppose Contra aid, with the exception of Gore, who wants to keep help down to a minimal humanitarian level.

Bush is the only candidate who could be damaged by allegations of direct complicity in the Iran/Contra scandal, but he has been protected from excessive harm because the level of his involvement remains in doubt. (In the early stage of the campaign there were also rumours of links between him and the controversial military ruler of Panama, General Manuel Noriega, who had been charged with drug offences in the United States. Here again, however, nothing was proved.)

As for the Iranian aspect of the Iran/Contra deal, the candidates of both parties are unanimous in denouncing arms supplies while Iran continues to sponsor terrorism. There were Democrats who doubted President Reagan's wisdom in dispatching American warships to the Gulf, to protect international shipping from being caught up in the conflict between Iraq and Iran. But since the ships appear to be fulfilling their function without provoking dangerous incidents, the policy now has few critics. The more central Middle East problem, the enduring contest between Israel and the Palestinians, came to the fore as an issue during the New York Democratic primary in April. Jesse Jackson has in the past advocated negotiating with the Palestine Liberation Organisation and aroused Jewish hostility during the 1984 campaign, when he characterised New York as 'Hymietown' – seen as an anti-Semitic slur. Of the three leading Democrats, Albert Gore was the most fervently pro-Israeli and was rewarded with the endorsement of Ed Koch, the city's Jewish mayor.

THE SIX KEY ISSUES: WHERE THEY STAND

	Higher taxes	*Welfare spending*	*INF treaty*	*Star Wars*	*Allow abortion*	*Contra aid*
REPUBLICANS						
Bush	No	Control	For	Deploy	Limited	Yes
Dole	Few	Maintain	For	Deploy	Limited	Yes
Kemp	No	Reform	Against	Deploy	No	Yes
Robertson	No	Reform	Against	Deploy	No	Yes
DEMOCRATS						
Dukakis	Few	Improve	For	Against	Yes	No
Gephardt	Maybe	Increase	For	Against	Yes	No
Gore	Maybe	Increase	For	Research	Yes	Minimal
Jackson	Yes	Increase	For	Research	Yes	No
Simon	Yes	Reform	For	Against	Yes	No

7

1988 – The Candidates

By the time election year dawned the 'great communicator' had little more to say. Ronald Reagan gave the impression that it would be a relief for him – as it would be for many of America's friends – when, on 20 January 1989, he could walk out of the Oval Office for the last time. It was not just the Iran/Contra scandal and the continuing questions about how much the President knew. The combination of that and his inevitable ageing, together with the departure of many of his former aides and confidants, meant that the mood emanating from the White House was one of impotence rather than assurance.

The last year in office of a President who cannot be re-elected – a 'lame duck' President – is often thus. On the credit side, however, was the arms limitation agreement with the Russians in December 1987. And through it all Reagan managed to maintain his personal popularity with millions of Americans: a phenomenon that George Bush, as his Vice-President, was able to exploit in the primaries.

In January 1988 the President attempted to set an upbeat mood for his final year in his penultimate State of the Union address, saying he did not accept that 1988 would see the last of anything. He appeared to believe that if Congress would approve of his plans to give more aid to the Contra rebels, his presidency would be vindicated. But Congress stood firm and, to make things worse, economic problems closed in. He made fewer breezy wisecracks as he climbed into his helicopter bound for his Camp David weekends. There were in any case not as many newshounds there to listen out for them. By now nearly all the nation's political pundits and reporters – an estimated 3,000 of them, increasing all the time – were in Iowa and New Hampshire, searching for fresh adjectives to convey the bitter cold, as well as for clues about who the next President would be.

The contest had in fact been under way for months already, since early 1987. Both sides were starting from a clean sheet, for it was the first time for twenty years that the incumbent President was not up for re-election. The Republicans had a Vice-President in George Bush and he was their early favourite. By the start of election year their nomination appeared to be a contest between him and Senator Robert Dole of Kansas.

The Democrats, still in disarray following the 1984 landslide despite gains in Congress, had no idea where to turn. Numerous hopefuls dipped their toes into the water. Some pulled them out almost instantly while others teetered on the edge, undecided. The contenders who emerged from the ruck were so little known outside Washington and their home states that they became known as the 'seven dwarfs'. (They were Snow White and the seven dwarfs while it looked as though Representative Patricia Schroeder was going to join, and they became the 'six pack' during Gary Hart's first temporary withdrawal.) Voters were anxiously searching for a sign that one of the dwarfs would be transformed miraculously into a giant but, as in a horse race, a large field was a sign that there was no one runner with outstanding claims. Equally, as in a horse race, there had to be an ultimate winner, although not necessarily from among the early contestants. The conditions of the race did not rule out late entries.

REPUBLICANS

George Bush, the Vice-President, would have been an almost certain choice for his party's nomination from the beginning were it not for two considerations: the Iran/Contra affair and the 'wimp factor'. He had, heaven knows, worked assiduously enough for it. He first set his sights on the White House in 1980. Although he had once been an ally of the right-wing Arizona Senator Barry Goldwater, by now he was seen as representing the moderate branch of the party, and did well enough in the early 1980 primaries and caucuses to make it appear for a while that he might defeat Reagan for the nomination. His performance during that campaign convinced Reagan that, in order to unite his party, he ought to choose Bush as his vice-presidential running-mate, rather than someone whose philosophy was closer to his own. From that moment Bush became a loyal Reagan supporter – even of the low-tax economic policy, which he had denounced during the primaries as 'voodoo economics'.

Born in 1924, Bush comes from a New England family – his father was a Senator for Connecticut. He distinguished himself as, reputedly, the youngest pilot in the Pacific sector in World War Two, completing a bombing mission from an aircraft carrier even after being hit by Japanese gunfire. After the war he graduated from Yale, where he was captain of baseball. Then he moved to Texas and made a substantial amount of money in the oil business. He represented Texas in the House of Representatives for four years before being chosen by President Nixon in 1971 as US ambassador at the United Nations in New York, where he served for two years.

Nixon, at the start of his second term in 1973, appointed Bush as chairman of the Republican National Committee – replacing Robert Dole, who ceded the post unwillingly. That initiated a long-term rivalry between the two men. In 1974 Bush was made the first head of the US liaison office in China, paving the way for full diplomatic relations between the two countries. In 1976 President Ford appointed him director of the Central Intelligence Agency. He performed all his jobs competently, without ever making a tremendous impact, although David Broder, a *Washington Post* columnist, may have been a mite unfair when he wrote that Bush had 'risen to higher and higher appointive posts by pleasing, flattering and serving men in power'. Married with five children, Bush has made two unsuccessful bids for a seat in the Senate.

As Vice-President, he found it as impossible as his predecessors in the post to stake out an independent position for himself, despite the ritual declaration by the President that he wanted his deputy to have real power. He often represented the country at state funerals – prompting the Reverend Jesse Jackson to observe during a televised debate that he had met as many live world statesmen as Bush had met dead ones. It was clear that Bush was willing to be patient and sit out his eight years as a loyal servant of Reagan in the hope of inheriting his office, despite the record that shows that no serving Vice-President has been elected to the White House for 150 years.

At the end of 1986, when the Iran/Contra scandal broke, it seemed that Bush's years of patience might have been wasted. Partly because of his former service in the CIA, it was assumed that he must have played a central role in the decisions to sell arms to Iran in the hope of gaining the release of American hostages and to use the profits for the benefit of the Contra rebels in Nicaragua. The investigations by the Tower Commission and by Congress did not, however, pin anything specific on him. He maintained that he had known of the arms supplies but not of the hostage link, that he had voiced reservations and that if he *had* been aware of the whole picture he would not have approved, because he is against bargaining with hostage-takers. He refused, however, to give further details, maintaining that his discussions with the President were confidential. 'I'm not a kiss-and-teller,' he said.

In December, 1987, the congressional investigators released a 1986 memorandum from Admiral John Poindexter, the national security adviser, describing Bush as 'solid' in his support for the Iran arms deal, in contrast to George Shultz, the Secretary of State, and Caspar Weinberger, Secretary of Defense, who expressed their opposition volubly. The following month the *Washington Post* published a report maintaining that Bush had attended several dozen meetings at which the deals were discussed. He was said to have known as much as the President about the details and to have expressed no reservations. Certainly his denials appeared to conflict with his frequent assertion that he was a participant in all major White House decisions. But his version received support from Donald Regan, the former White House chief of staff, who said Bush had used 'graphic language' to express doubts about the Iran arms policy.

In the early months of 1987, Bush was easily leading the field of Republican contenders. Opinion polls showed that he had the support of thirty-eight per cent of Republicans, twice as many as his closest rival, Senator Dole. By the late summer, though, the gap had narrowed: Bush had lost four points and Dole had gained the same amount. Jack Kemp, the conservative New York congressman, was a distant third.

Bush used his position as Vice-President to good advantage. In the autumn of 1987 he made a ten-day tour of six European countries, ostensibly to reassure the United States' allies that their interests would be protected in the forthcoming deal with the Russians on intermediate-range missiles. In fact it was a thinly-disguised campaign ruse to establish his credentials as an international statesman. It was not altogether successful. As soon as he returned he had to apologise for an off-the-cuff remark to the effect that Russian car workers were more productive than those in Detroit. (That did not prevent him gaining an impressive majority in Michigan, whose Republicans selected their convention delegates in January, before the Iowa caucuses.)

The week after his return from Europe he formally declared his candidacy and in doing so gave what might have been a rash hostage to fortune. 'I am not going to raise your taxes – period,' he pledged. He did not say how, in that case, he was going to achieve the balanced budget that he advocated: but he was by no means the only candidate to fudge on such details.

The two most damaging words used about the Vice-President were 'wimp' and 'preppy'. David Broder's point that he had been appointed more often than elected to his senior jobs – which made him beholden to the person who chose him – contributed to the image of an insubstantial time-server with no firm views of his own. He found an effective answer to that in the televised debates, saying that he did not regard loyalty as a character defect. After the first such debate between all six Republican contenders in the autumn of 1987, the opinion polls showed that Bush was judged the winner. Yet the impression lingered of an over-grown college student, lacking assertiveness. His opponents plugged away at that theme, with Dole, as a long-serving senator, asserting that he, Dole, was running on 'a record not a resumé'. Word from the Democratic Party was that they thought they would stand a better chance of winning an election against Bush than against Dole.

Bush's weaknesses include his tendency towards pettiness in debate and making ill-considered remarks that he later regrets. In 1984 he was much criticised after a debate with Geraldine Ferraro, the Democratic vice-presidential candi-date, when he commented, 'I whipped her ass' – perhaps over-compensating for the wimp factor. After that he was given a reduced role in the campaign. But in January 1988 he used this inflammable streak to good advantage in a live television interview with the formidable Dan Rather in the prime-time news bulletin on CBS, one of the major television networks. When Rather tried to nail him down on the Iran/Contra question, Bush counter-attacked, weighed into Rather and claimed he had been misled about the subject of the interview. Rather panicked and public reaction showed that Bush had done a lot to erase suggestions of wimpishness. Some, though, remained unconvinced. In a cruel barb, the *Boston Globe* likened him to 'every woman's first husband'. And in a *Time* magazine poll, seventy-nine per cent of respondents said they thought Bush knew more about the arms deal than he admitted and more people, even Republicans, trusted Rather than trusted Bush.

The Washington summit in December 1987 allowed the Vice-President to strengthen the point that he was the man with experience in foreign affairs. Pictures of him fraternising with Mikhail Gorbachev, the Soviet leader, were used in his campaign commercials in Iowa. He gave uncompromising support to the intermediate-range missile treaty, although it was opposed by conservative Republicans. Dole dithered over the treaty for a while before deciding in its favour. (As Senate Republican leader, it would be his task to steer it through the upper house.) All the other contenders expressed reservations about it.

Bush began the campaign as warm favourite but had to overcome opposition from the right wing of the party, who felt disillusioned by Reagan's overtures towards the Russians and regarded Bush as an accomplice to betrayal. When it came to the point, much would depend on how deep that disillusion ran. After Iowa, things did not look promising. He came a poor third, behind Dole and the preacher Pat Robertson. Opinion polls in New Hampshire showed Dole whittling his lead away. But he campaigned hard in the New England state, adopting a more rugged image. He wore casual jackets and peaked caps and was photographed at the controls of farm equipment. He beat Dole by a convincing nine per cent – thirty-eight to twenty-nine – and went into Super Tuesday with a fair wind behind him.

That fair wind blew up to gale force as soon as the polls closed on 8 March. He came top in all but one of the sixteen primaries – the odd one out was Washington state, which went to Pat Robertson. He won more than half the total vote and, barring unforeseen disasters, seemed certain to be the candidate. Dole's withdrawal at the end of March made it inevitable. Discussion among the pundits was now centred on who would be his vice-presidential running-mate. He won because he represented continuity with a President who, despite his failings, remained popular in his party.

Pat Robertson is the real maverick in the Republican race, the only candidate who is not a politician – although his father was a conservative senator for Virginia. A 58-year-old television evangelist, his reputation is based on the Christian Broadcasting Network (CBN), a cable network that he established in 1960 and which now has twenty-five million subscribers, producing an annual revenue of $200 million. He was an evangelist in the 'charismatic' tradition, claiming miracle cures and conversions and raising millions of dollars from supporters. In one memorable broadcast he claimed that God, answering his prayers, had diverted a hurricane away from his church. He stood down from CBN when he announced his candidacy and also resigned his position as a minister in the Southern Baptist Church, although contributions from his flock ensured that his was one of the best funded of the primary campaigns.

Despite the fact that his television commercials play down his career as an evangelist, he campaigns primarily on moral issues. In his speeches he describes his vision of America as 'a city set on a hill, a light of righteousness for all the peoples of the world to come to, one nation under God'. He speaks out passionately against abortion, both on moral grounds and for the sake of keeping up the birthrate. He espouses family values and talks about getting 'radical homosexuals' off the streets. He has even claimed that God told him to run for the presidency, and that he would challenge communism even inside the Soviet Union, not flinching from war if he thought America's survival depended on it. He thinks the 'eastern liberal foreign policy establishment' have sold out American interests.

Part of his early success sprung from the fact that his rivals thought it would be unseemly and counter-productive to attack him as fiercely as they did the professional politicians. His campaign survived a number of revelations that would have harmed any of the others. Doubts were cast on his claims about his record in the Korean War; there were questions about his financial backing and it was revealed that the first of his four children had been born out of wedlock. He admitted that last charge, adding that as a youth he had indulged in 'wine, women and song on several continents'.

But he did well enough in the Iowa straw polls in the autumn of 1987 to establish himself as a serious contender. And after a persuasive performance in a televised debate in Houston that October, a poll of viewers said he had come out second best overall, behind Bush but ahead of Dole, Kemp and the others. In terms of 'presence, charisma and attractiveness' he was judged number one. He was looking sufficiently dangerous for a group of regular Republicans to start a campaign called ABR – Anyone But Robertson.

His first setback came in the Michigan conventions – the first Republican delegate-selection process of the year – where he had been expected to do well. In the event Bush beat him and all the other contenders easily. He needed a reasonable showing in Iowa and New Hampshire to set his campaign up for Super Tuesday, when he was expected to do well in the south. Iowa worked out well for him. He came a good second there to Dole with twenty-five per cent. But in New Hampshire he slipped to only ten per cent. A disappointing Super Tuesday resulted in just one victory – in the western state of Washington – and only thirteen per cent of the votes overall. By then it seemed as if nobody could stop Bush, certainly not Robertson. But although he stopped campaigning he kept his name in the lists, hoping to exert an influence at the New Orleans convention.

Dropouts

Robert Dole was running second – often a quite distant second – to Bush throughout the months of pre-primary jockeying for position. But with his support never dropping far below twenty per cent he was always just in with a chance, waiting to pounce if the Vice-President should falter. He represented Washington experience – something that President Reagan and his predecessor Jimmy Carter had lacked. He was known as an effective and persuasive manipulator of his congressional colleagues in the Lyndon Johnson tradition.

First elected to the House of Representatives for his native Kansas in 1960, when he was thirty-seven, Dole won a Senate seat after eight years and has held on to it since then. He was chairman of the Senate finance committee, then became majority leader in 1985 and minority leader two years later when the Democrats gained control. He was chairman of the Republican National Committee from 1971 to 1973, when he was replaced by Bush. In 1976 Gerald Ford selected him as his vice-presidential running mate, but they were beaten by Carter and Mondale. In 1980 he was briefly a candidate for the presidential nomination, but pulled out when he could see things were going Reagan's way.

In the imprecise political spectrum of Republican politics, Dole is seen as being to the right of Bush, but not an extreme conservative. On details of policy, the two scarcely differ. Both were campaigning on the need to reduce the budget deficit to help strengthen the dollar but neither was specific about how this could be done. Dole was always likely to do better than Bush in Iowa, because he comes from a neigh-bouring farming state. He supported the farmers on issues such as allowing exports of surplus grain to the Soviet Union. ('Sell 'em anything they can't shoot back at you,' was how he put it.)

Dole makes much of his humble beginnings in Russell, a small Kansas town where he worked at the soda fountain of the drugstore after school. His father was a mechanic who also ran a cream and eggs stall: local farmers would bring their produce to him for sale. He chose Russell to make the formal declaration of his candidacy in November 1987, saying: 'I offer the strength and determination, moulded in America's small-town heartland and tempered during a career of public service, to bring common-sense answers to the complex problems facing America in its third century.'

At the same ceremony, in a melodramatic scene, he accepted a $100,000 campaign contribution in a cigar box which, he said, was the very one used by the citizens of Russell in 1945 for the collection to help pay for three years and three months he had to spend in hospital following a terrible war wound he received in Italy. He lost a kidney and remains unable to use his right arm: he holds a pen in it to deter well-wishers from shaking hands. Balancing that physical disability, though, are his face and voice, both reminiscent of Humphrey Bogart.

Twice married, Dole has a daughter from his first marriage and a valuable asset in his second wife, Elizabeth, thirteen years his junior. A formidable southerner, she resigned in July 1987 as President Reagan's Secretary of Transportation (the only female cabinet member) to assist her husband's campaign. He was damaged, however, a few weeks before the Iowa caucuses, by allegations of irregularities in connection with the 'blind trust' established for Mrs Dole's financial holdings when she was appointed to the cabinet. As a result, one of his aides resigned. Whether or not any serious indiscretion was committed, the suggestion of wheeler-dealing conflicted with the image he was trying to establish of a humble country boy, comparing himself with Bush, the New England aristocrat, the 'poor little rich boy', as Dole's aides had taken to calling him.

In his 1976 vice-presidential campaign, Dole had been cast in a combative role such as Spiro Agnew had played for Richard Nixon. While President Ford remained statesman-like, so as not to compromise the dignity of his office, Dole made some mean, abrasive speeches criticising the challenger, Jimmy Carter. He has a sharp wit and some of his jokes can be barbed and sarcastic.

Recognising that this can lead to misunderstandings on the campaign trail, he went on a course in New York to soften his image. 'We don't want any of that hatchet stuff,' he told reporters. But he still could not resist entering into some bad-tempered exchanges with Bush in the first weeks of election year about whether Dole's experience in Congress qualified him better for the presidency than Bush's more varied record. Angered by the role of Bush's campaign team in circulating the story about his wife's 'blind trust', Dole retaliated by seeking answers from the Vice-President about his role in the Iran/Contra affair, sensing that this was the issue on which his chief opponent was most vulnerable.

Dole is almost as unpopular with hard-line conservatives as Bush. As Senate leader, he was obliged to make too many compromises for their liking, in particular by watering down Reagan's low-tax policy in order to get budget measures through. He was also one of the architects of the 1985 farm subsidy legislation, which benefits his Kansas constituents but costs the country $29 billion a year. Dole's best chance would have come if Bush had fared poorly in the early primaries, when the moderate wing of the party would rally round him as the least of the remaining evils, the means of preventing the nomination going to one of the more extremist contenders, such as Jack Kemp or Pat Robertson. Recognising this, during his campaign Dole tempered his conservatism with compassion for the nation's neediest, saying that the budget must not be balanced at their expense – nor at the expense of taxpayers.

Dole did better than expected in Iowa, with thirty-seven per cent of the vote, but worse than he had hoped in New Hampshire. His snappy temper began to rear its head again in the run-up to Super Tuesday and this probably contributed to his poor showing, first in South Carolina and then on 8 March itself, when he won only twenty-four per cent of the vote to Bush's fifty-six, and did not come first in a single state – not even his wife's home territory of North Carolina. From then on, his bid for the White House was doomed to failure. He withdrew two weeks after the Illinois poll on 15 March.

Pierre (Pete) du Pont began and ended his campaign as a little-known rank outsider from Delaware, one of the smallest states of the union. A poll taken by *Time* magazine in September showed that only fifteen per cent of Republicans had ever heard of him and only two per cent made him their first choice for President. He had been a congressman between 1971 and 1977 and Governor of Delaware for eight years after that. At fifty-two, he and Jack Kemp were the two youngest Republican contenders – as well as among the most conservative. Married with four children, he is a member of the family that founded the giant du Pont chemical firm, which exerts tremendous influence in Delaware.

His policies were not only conservative but novel. He wanted to cut federal spending by ending subsidies for farmers, closing 100 military bases, replacing welfare programmes with a compulsory work scheme and privatising pensions and social security, allowing people to opt out of the system if they wished. He also advocated drug tests for all high school students: those found to have been using the substances would forfeit their driving licences.

His advocacy of ending farm subsidies made him no friends in Iowa, where he won only seven per cent of the Republican vote. In the pre-primary televised debates he sought to capitalise on the fact that at least his policies were clearly defined, unlike that of the all-things-to-all-men front runners. He was rewarded by George Bush characterising his ideas for social security as 'nutty'. Voters seemed to agree. Except in his home state, he was not much more familiar to the public after the opening contests than before. He had been the first Republican to declare himself a candidate for the 1988 nomination, announcing it in June 1986. He was the second (after Haig) to withdraw, pulling out after scoring eleven per cent in New Hampshire, just above Robertson but, crucially, two per cent below his conservative rival Kemp.

Alexander Haig would have been among the favourites if foreign policy credentials were the criteria. A former general of sixty-three, he fought in the Korean War just after graduating from West Point, and later commanded a battalion in Vietnam. In 1973, in a vain attempt to restore some dignity to the White House after the Watergate resignations, President Nixon appointed him his chief of staff. His contribution to the gaiety of nations in that role was the creation of a strange brand of military-style jargon that came to be known as 'Haigspeak'. He mangled the language and created such monstrous phrases as a 'vortex of cruciality'.

When Nixon resigned, Haig was made supreme military commander of NATO. He left that post in 1978 and went into business as president of the United Technologies Corporation, until President Reagan brought him back into politics as his first Secretary of State. He left in 1982 following reports of disagreements with members of the White House staff: their relationship never recovered from the debacle just after the assassination attempt on the President, when Haig told the world that he was taking charge.

His campaign for the presidency began early in 1987 but never caught the imagination of the media or the public and he found it hard to raise money for television advertising. This was probably because he concentrated on foreign affairs at a time when the United States was worried about its internal problems. He called for a summit conference on the future of the world economy and warned that the Reagan administration's vision of a world without nuclear weapons took insufficient account of Europe's vulnerability to the evil intentions of the Russians. In pre-primary debates he said that the agreement to cut intermediate-range missiles would be 'a major step towards World War Three'. But his manner was over-assertive and his warnings fell on deaf ears.

One man whose support Haig did command – though it was of dubious value – was his former boss, ex-President Nixon. In a memorandum to a Republican Party consultant in the summer of 1987, Nixon wrote: 'If by election day the question uppermost in the voters' minds is which of the candidates could best handle himself one-to-one with the most able Soviet leader since Stalin, Mikhail Gorbachev, Haig would have to be their first choice.'

But that did not reflect the priorities of the electorate. Haig had not made much effort in Iowa and made no showing there. The opinion polls had him doing poorly in New Hampshire, too, and four days before the primary he withdrew from the race and threw his support behind Dole, who had won Iowa and seemed to be about to snatch New Hampshire from Bush, Haig's old rival. Haig hoped his switch would tip the scales in Dole's favour – but the move failed, for Bush won New Hampshire and did not look back.

Jack Kemp was the initial favourite of right-wing politicians who felt that Reagan had not properly implemented the low-tax supply-side economic theories on which he had been elected – not as thoroughly, for example, as Margaret Thatcher had done in Britain. A congressman for Buffalo, New York, Kemp came to prominence in the late 1970s as a co-sponsor of a tax-reduction bill that was based on the

'Laffer curve' – a theory that held that if you cut taxes to a critical level you boost the economy to the extent that you are actually *increasing* the amount of revenue that goes to the exchequer. Despite the fact that the Reagan tax cuts had the effect of increasing the budget deficit and weakening the dollar, this view is still strongly held among conservatives. Kemp now goes further and advocates a return to the gold standard.

Aged fifty-two, married with four children, the handsome Kemp was a professional footballer for thirteen years, a quarterback with the San Diego Chargers and the Buffalo Bills. First elected to the House of Representatives in 1970, he takes right-wing positions on issues other than taxes, speaking out firmly in favour of aid to the Contras, for less government involvement in everyday life and against the missile treaty. Kemp was running third or fourth in most of the early opinion polls and he made little impact in the televised debates.

In Iowa and New Hampshire, his scores averaged only twelve per cent and by Super Tuesday he was down to five per cent – a long way last of the four candidates. Two days later he dropped out of the race and said he would not seek a further term in Congress. The question now was whether he would throw in his lot with Bush in the hope of being invited to become Vice-President, adding conservative ballast to the ticket.

Non-runners

Midway through a President's term there are scores of politicians being mentioned as potential contenders to succeed him. Many of them took an early look at the field in 1988 and declared emphatically that they would not join it. In the case of the Democrats, not all of them necessarily meant it. The Republicans probably did and these are some of the more notable among them:

Howard Baker. Senator from Tennessee who made his name on the committee investigating Watergate. Briefly a candidate in 1980. Replaced Donald Regan as White House chief of staff after Iran/Contra revelations. On the moderate wing of the party.

Patrick Buchanan. Right-winger and long-time ally and adviser to Richard Nixon, both before and during his presidency. Wrote combative speeches for Nixon and Vice-President Agnew.

Jean Kirkpatrick. Conservative academic, formerly a Democrat, appointed by Ronald Reagan as his ambassador to the United Nations because of her views on the need for the USA to support right-wing regimes, even authoritarian ones. At the UN she won respect from right-wing Republicans for her robustness under pressure from Third World delegates. She left the administration when she was not offered the post of Secretary of State or National Security Adviser. Her name was enthusiastically touted on the right in the autumn of 1987 but after saying she was 'seriously considering' a candidacy she declared in October that she was not running. She was still being mentioned, though, as a vice-presidential possibility. Just before Super Tuesday she endorsed Dole, possibly hoping to be his running-mate if he won the nomination. But it did him no good.

Paul Laxalt. Conservative former senator for Nevada. Early associate and close friend of Reagan and an architect of his successful run for the presidency. Declared himself in the race in the summer of 1987 but out of it by the autumn.

DEMOCRATS

Michael Dukakis is serving his third term as Governor of Massachusetts. A state representative since 1962, he was a surprising winner of the governorship in 1974, lost it in 1978, won it back in 1982 and was re-elected in 1986. His position gave him two initial advantages over the others. First, the state's economic revival (see page 112) gave him something to boast about and secondly it adjoins New Hampshire, which meant he was sure of local support in the all-important February primary. The son of Greek immigrants, married with three children, Dukakis, fifty-four, is a liberal, but not of the free-spending kind. As governor, he managed to balance the state's budget while at the same time cutting taxes – achievements of which he was not slow to remind the electors.

His plan for doing the same at the federal level was regarded by the commentators as unsound. He said that stricter enforcement could ensure payment of at least a third of the $110 billion worth of federal taxes assessed but unpaid every year. With part of the money he would establish a fund to create jobs and induce economic growth, aiming to take people off the welfare rolls, and he would spend more on education. In the autumn of 1987 he was running second of the Democratic candidates in most national polls, behind Jesse Jackson. In a poll of Washington officials, he was the choice of nearly half – possibly because he is not Washington based and they were less familiar with any foibles.

Then his campaign was damaged by a rebounding 'dirty trick' on Senator Joseph Biden, a rival for liberal support. Members of the Dukakis campaign team prepared a video tape showing that Senator Biden had copied parts of his speeches from those of Neil Kinnock, leader of the British Labour Party. The embarrassment caused Biden to withdraw from the race (see page 174) but then two members of Dukakis's own staff resigned when the ruse was pinned on them, and Dukakis himself apologised.

He played no personal role in the distribution of the tape and it would indeed have been uncharacteristic of him, for he seldom indulges in personal abuse of his rivals. That would conflict with the reserved, almost colourless manner that is the despair of his image-makers. He is introspective and, in public, unemotional: a bit of a cold fish. Yet with that lack of personal magnetism goes a tough, stubborn streak. Massachusetts politicians have learned, often to their cost, that once his mind is made up on a subject he is virtually impossible to dislodge.

He has a streak of populism about him. In Iowa he stayed on farms during campaign trips, while the other candidates based themselves at local hotels. But as a New Englander he found it hard to overcome the generally austere and prissy image of the region that prevails in the mid-west – and indeed in the south, where the Super Tuesday primaries were being held. He declared for the presidency only after Governor Cuomo of New York said he would not run. Their political views are similar but, even after many months of campaigning, the New Englander had scarcely begun to attain the New Yorker's national visibility.

After a respectable third place in Iowa, though, Dukakis justified his position as favourite in New Hampshire, which adjoins his home state. There he gained thirty-seven per cent of the vote and finished well ahead of the second-placed Richard Gephardt. He also won convincingly in Minnesota. These early successes made him look like a potential winner and helped him raise money, which he used to set up what was recognised as the most effective organisation of all the Democrats. Much depended on how the south took to him. The fact that his wife Kitty is Jewish was a plus factor in some southern states, especially Florida, which he won. He also took Texas, with its 173 convention votes. Overall on Super Tuesday, he was in a virtual three-way tie with Jackson and Gore, who was planning on a strong late finish. Gradually it began to dawn on the pundits that, of the declared contenders, Dukakis was the most likely to be the nominee; but the band-wagon effect took a while to make itself felt. In Illinois, he could finish only third to two 'local' candidates, Paul Simon and Jesse Jackson. Michigan, a week later, was even worse. He had been expected to do well in this northern industrial state but was convincingly defeated by Jackson, who now had as many committed delegates as the Massachusetts Governor. But Dukakis fought back in Connecticut, Colorado and Wisconsin and went into the vital New York primary with a useful lead. An impressive victory there meant that he was virtually certain to go to the Atlanta convention with the most committed delegates, although this did not automatically mean that he would be the candidate.

Jesse Jackson occupied the unusual position of leading the opinion polls among Democratic possibles for much of 1987, but being written off as having no hope of winning the nomination. The common explanation for his good showing in the early polls was that none of the other candidates was anything like as well known nationally. The accepted view that America is 'not ready' for a black President is partly based on demographics: only twelve per cent of the population is black. Since most of those who vote are Democrats, his chance of nomination by the party would be higher than that, but still remote, if race were the only criterion. In 1984 he won twelve per cent of the delegates to the convention, with eighteen per cent of the primary and caucus votes. Three-quarters of the blacks who turned out in the primaries voted for him, but only five per cent of whites, according to a survey in the *New York Times*.

It is not just his colour, though, that makes the 46-year-old Jackson an unlikely winner. Politically, he is perceived as occupying a position further to the left than is generally presumed to be electable. His former support of the militant Black Muslim movement and his sympathy with the Arab cause in the Middle East make it hard for him to attract Jewish votes. In polls measuring the negative as well as the positive responses inspired by the candidates, he invariably came close to the top of the negative column.

Jackson, born to an unmarried mother in South Carolina, has been a civil rights activist since the 1960s, when Martin Luther King put him in charge of Operation Breadbasket, a campaign to raise the economic conditions of poor blacks. His claim to have been at King's side when he was assassinated is disputed by King's family. A magnetic and forceful public speaker, in 1971 he formed his own organisation in Chicago, Operation PUSH (People United to Save Humanity), which has put pressure on businesses nationwide to hire more black people. In 1983 he created the National Rainbow Coalition, embracing many civil rights groups. He has been married for twenty-five years and has five children. Like the other church-man in the contest, the Republicans' Pat Robertson, he married after his first child was conceived – a fact he admitted when a newspaper uncovered it, and which did not seem to dent his support.

Recognising that he needs white votes if his candidacy is to be anything more than a brave gesture, Jackson has moder-ated some of his views. On foreign affairs he is to the right of some of his rivals: for instance, he favours research on the Star Wars defence system (although not its deployment). Domestically, though, his policies are more radical: two-thirds reductions in military spending and extra taxes on the wealthy, all going to increase welfare provision.

Although he had been campaigning since early in 1987, Jackson spent far fewer dollars than his rivals (see table page 187). Instead of buying television advertising time, he relied on news coverage of his electrifying stump speeches, with repetitive rhetoric and pregnant pauses, based on the tech-niques of revivalist preachers. One theme he has addressed repeatedly in his campaign is his passionate opposition to drug abuse, which particularly affects young black people but is also of great concern to whites. He discourages endorse-ment from far left groups, knowing that they are bad for his image.

Despite his insistence that he is contending for the nomina-tion itself, realistically the best he can hope for is to go to the Atlanta convention with many more delegates than last time and enough strength to influence the choice of candidate and the platform. His scores of nine and eight per cent in Iowa and New Hampshire were in line with what had been expected but he did surprisingly well in Minnesota. Although there are comparatively few blacks in the state, he won twenty per cent of the vote, suggesting that he could win support among white voters. Certainly he appeared to be winning more white support this time than in 1984. In the south he received important help from Bert Lance, a Georgia banker and former member of President Carter's cabinet. He won five states there on Super Tuesday, enough to assure him of a strong voice in the final selection.

The next two contests, in Illinois and Michigan, marked the high point of his campaign. He did so well amongst black and white voters that, for the first time, his chance of the nomination was taken seriously. In Illinois, his adopted state, he won 31 per cent of the vote – behind the 'favourite son' Paul Simon but well ahead of Michael Dukakis, who scored only 17 per cent. In Michigan he trounced Dukakis again, by 54 per cent to 29.

His star began to wane, comparatively speaking, in Wisconsin, where the positions were roughly, reversed – Dukakis 48 per cent and Jackson 28. He now needed to beat Dukakis in New York to have any chance of gaining a majority of convention delegates, but was unable to overcome the hostility of Jewish voters. He had, however, certainly established himself as a powerful voice in Democratic politics – the first black leader to reach such a position.

Dropouts

Bruce Babbitt, Governor of Arizona from 1978 to 1987, had been a dark horse candidate ever since he began campaigning in New Hampshire and Iowa early in 1987. Short of money and initially of organisation, handicapped by a less than fluent public speaking style, he had little going in his favour until the reporters assigned to the primaries decided that, partly because of his flaws and partly because of his self-deprecating wit, he was a more interesting candidate than most. His poll ratings were consistently in single figures, which meant that he had little to lose by being the only contender to make the uncompromising and unpopular declaration that taxes had to be increased if the budget was to be balanced.

Born in 1938 to a successful Catholic business family in Flagstaff, Arizona, Babbitt was an active campaigner for civil rights and social causes and took part in the freedom march in

Selma in 1965. He was involved in President Johnson's anti-poverty programme and, after practising as a lawyer in Phoenix, he was elected Arizona's attorney-general in 1974. Three years later he became Governor of the state by an odd combination of circumstances, when one governor resigned, his successor died and Babbitt was next in line. He won re-election twice and managed to persuade a suspicious Republican legislature to enact many of the social policies he wanted. He is married with two children.

His candidacy was often compared to that of Jimmy Carter, another little-known state governor who won the nomination by doggedly applying himself to campaigning in the primary states. But perhaps because many still remembered the Carter presidency he made little impact on the public, although more on the media. (One of his TV commercials consisted merely of reading favourable press comments about him.) At the end of January, he began to climb slowly in the polls as the media's enthusiasm for him filtered down to the electorate, but the surge was short-lived. He polled six per cent in Iowa and five per cent in New Hampshire, then pulled out.

Joe Biden, a 44-year-old senator from Delaware, was the first declared candidate on either side to drop out of the contest (with the exception of Gary Hart, who dropped out only to climb back). None of the commentators thought Biden had any real chance of the nomination but his withdrawal, in September 1987, came in faintly ludicrous circumstances that caused particular amusement in Britain. In a debate at the Iowa State Fair in August, Biden included a passage of rhetoric that began: 'Why is it that Joe Biden is the first in his family ever to go to university? Is it because our fathers and mothers were not bright?' He went on to speak of his ancestors' toughness, how they had worked hard in the mines of Pennsylvania and played football afterwards. He concluded by saying that the reason they had not advanced was because they had no platform to stand on.

The passage was in fact lifted, with suitable regional altera-tions, from a speech that Neil Kinnock, leader of the British

Labour Party, had made during that summer's general election campaign. Biden had not credited Kinnock with it and for two weeks nobody noticed; until members of the Dukakis campaign team (see above) released a video comparing the two passages. Although Biden's campaign had made little impact until then – in terms of public recognition he was the most insignificant of the 'seven dwarfs' – he was thought to be a potential rival to Dukakis for liberal votes.

Reporters followed up the 'plagiarism' evidence with further suggestions that Biden had on occasion copied the speeches of President Kennedy and his brothers, and had even been involved in a comparable incident when a student at law school. Biden quit the race, promising to be back another year. But he did enjoy success in another area that summer. As chairman of the Senate judiciary committee he led the successful fight against President Reagan's plan to appoint the conservative judge Robert Bork to the Supreme Court. Reagan's second choice was rejected, too. Only at the third try did he pick a man acceptable to Congress. Biden came out of that affair with an increased reputation, but it was too late to affect the 1988 contest, in which he was no longer taking part.

Richard Gephardt, a congressman from St Louis, Missouri since 1977, is another populist. Drawing on the memory of his state's most celebrated son, President Harry Truman, he declared his candidacy at the railway station where Truman claimed victory after the election in 1948. Gephardt, forty-six, is married with three children. Politically, he is best known as a protectionist who gave his name to an amendment to a bill that would require America's trading partners to cut their surpluses by ten per cent a year or face retaliation. His most talked-about campaign commercial made the point well: it showed how a Chrysler car costing $10,000 in the United States sold for almost five times that amount in South Korea, because of high tariffs.

He also proposes a tax on imported oil to keep its price up, to the benefit of US producers. An active legislator, he introduced a tax reform bill into Congress and has some radical foreign policy views, among them support of the African National Congress in South Africa. Pressed in a televised debate about his lack of experience in foreign policy he pointed out that John Kennedy equally could point to no formal experience in that field but was able to face up to Nikita Krushchev, the Soviet leader. He was clearly trying to project a Kennedy-style image in all respects except for the former President's privileged background. In a race where the candidates vied with each other as to who could boast the humblest origins, Gephardt made much of the fact that his father was a milkman.

In Iowa he campaigned strongly on a plan to increase farm prices and quickly began to show well in the opinion polls. He portrayed himself as a rugged individualist and in his speeches he attacked 'the establishment' and 'corporate America' (shades of Jimmy Carter). Noting that it had been Iowa that established Hart as a viable contender in 1984, Gephardt spent more time in that state than any of his rivals, and as the primary approached his investment seemed to be paying off: he climbed to the top of the polls following the fading of Hart. As he did so, though, reporters, encouraged by his opponents, began investigating his Washington record further and found inconsistencies in it. On several issues he seemed to have changed his mind to fit in with the currently popular view – the majority view that could win him the nomination. Although this 'flip-flop' tendency was stressed in many published profiles, it did not appear to affect his chances in the early stages of the campaign.

Gephardt was staking everything on a good result in Iowa to attract the funds he needed to carry on, and he got it, coming top of the poll with thirty-one per cent, four ahead of Paul Simon. The impetus from that took him to a respectable second place to Dukakis in New Hampshire, with twenty per cent. He won South Dakota but came a bad fifth in Minnesota. Going into Super Tuesday, he and Dukakis seemed well ahead of the rest, but he faltered badly on that vital day, coming a poor fourth with thirteen per cent and winning only one state, Missouri. It was then a matter of time before he withdrew at the end of March, after another poor showing in Michigan.

Albert Gore, at thirty-nine the youngest candidate from either party (and he looks even younger), was also the only Democrat running from a southern state, following the July 1987 announcement by Senator Sam Nunn of Georgia that he would not be entering the lists. Elected as a congressman for Tennessee in 1976, Gore graduated to the Senate eight years later. His father had been a senator for three terms, which explains why Gore was born in Washington. After serving in the Vietnam war he became a journalist in Tennessee and also ran a building business. He underlined his youth by letting it be known that he keeps fit by running four miles every day, and his resemblance to Christopher Reeve, the actor who played Superman, does him no harm. He has four children and a wife who has campaigned against immoral lyrics in popular songs. (Among southern Democrats, this helped compensate for suggestions that he once had moderate tendencies.) He tried to stake out positions to the right of his rivals to appeal to the south, and on Super Tuesday won his reward.

Gore is an expert in science and technology. A member of the powerful Senate Armed Services Committee, he has specialised in arms control issues. He wants to cut spending on defence but insists that he will not countenance any weakening of America's military strength. He implies that because of his expertise he, unlike the other contenders, will be able to distinguish between those cuts that do weaken America and those that do not. He is against the deployment of the Star Wars strategic defence system and in favour of further arms reductions as long as they are mutual. Domestically, he opposes protectionism and advocates means-testing welfare benefits.

His strategy for the primaries was different from his rivals'. He recognised that, as a southerner, he would not do well in Iowa and New Hampshire. So, challenging the conventional wisdom and the lessons of the past, he decided to make no real effort there, visiting them only once in a while to denounce the system that placed so much emphasis on two such unrepresentative states. Instead, he concentrated his resources on the southern states for the Super Tuesday primaries on 8 March. This allowed Gephardt and Dukakis to steal the vital early headlines. The view among political commentators was that Gore would not get the nomination but was a natural for the vice-presidency, balancing the ticket of a northern candidate. He insisted, however, that he was in the contest for the top job, and his performance in the south reinforced that claim. He won five southern states plus Nevada and by the morning after Super Tuesday he was up with the front runners. But he dropped back when the campaign moved north again and bowed out after gaining only 10 per cent of the New York vote despite the endorsement of the Mayor, Ed Koch.

Gary Hart was initially the subject of much more press coverage than any other candidate from either party; but it was not the kind of coverage to do him any good and his chances dwindled with every fresh news story. In 1984 he had given a nasty shock to Walter Mondale, the favourite for the nomination, by doing well enough in Iowa and New Hampshire to make the former Vice-President recognise that he was in a contest. He had started campaigning early and for 1988 he used the same tactic, travelling around the primary and caucus states from the start of 1987. But in May of that year his campaign ground to an abrupt halt when the press revealed that he had spent the night with Donna Rice, a 29-year-old model from Miami, at his Washington townhouse.

Amid tales of other infidelities during his twenty-nine-year marriage, the tall, lean Hart, who is fifty-one, withdrew from the race and his campaign team dispersed. But just before Christmas 1987 he surprised everyone by announcing in New Hampshire that he was rejoining the contest. He had become frustrated on the sidelines and calculated that, in the continued absence of Mario Cuomo, Governor of New York, the other contenders would not be hard to beat. His children were also said to be urging him to run and his wife Lee stayed at his side, smiling bravely.

Hart was born and brought up in Kansas as a member of the Church of Nazarene, an offshoot of the Methodists with a rigid moral code. His surname at birth was Hartpence but he lopped off the final syllable to make it snappier. (The press also discovered embarrassingly that his official biography lopped a year off his age.)

His first role on the national political scene was as campaign manager to George McGovern in his doomed contest for the presidency in 1972. That established his political position on the left of the party and he was elected as a senator for Colorado two years later. In 1984, Mondale finally beat him by casting doubt on his reliability on the substance of policy. 'Where's the beef?' he asked, quoting a current advertisement for hamburgers.

Until the Donna Rice affair – which he compounded by initially denying that there was any impropriety – Hart had been favourite for the 1988 nomination. His December announcement that he would revive his candidacy was at first greeted with cynicism and some dismay. Many thought he was doing it simply to qualify for federal funds; he still owed money from his 1984 campaign. One Democrat said he was like a 'bastard cousin who shows up at the family reunion'. Yet, possibly because of the extent of the press coverage of his decision, he shot instantly to the top of the opinion polls. In a telephone poll done for *Time*, thirty per cent made him their choice, fifty-two per cent approved of his decision to re-enter the race and fifty-nine per cent agreed with Hart that the press had been unfair in investigating his private life. On the other hand, more than forty per cent thought he would make a suitable character for a soap opera.

Hart attacked the press for prying into his personal life and pointed out that he was not running for sainthood. 'We have never expected perfection in our leaders,' he asserted, maintaining that the power of his ideas overrode any personal failings. Those ideas included raising taxes to handle the

budget deficit (like Babbitt), better job training for young-
sters and reforming the armed services. But the public were
not convinced and he was short of money and staff to persuade them. His initial surge in the polls after his re-entry was
short-lived and his ratings sank further when he put up an
unimpressive performance in the year's first televised debate.
Shortly afterwards the *Miami Herald*, which had broken the
Donna Rice story, ran another report questioning whether
certain contributions to Hart's 1984 campaign had been in
breach of the election laws. He won no measurable support in
Iowa and came bottom of the poll with four per cent in New
Hampshire. On Super Tuesday he won only three per cent of
the vote and his withdrawal was inevitable.

Paul Simon was the Democrat who deviated most from the
image of the clean-cut, professional politician that has
seemed to be standard for the last two decades. At fifty-nine
the oldest of his party's contenders, he has oversized ears,
heavy spectacles and sports an out-of-fashion bow tie. He
conducts himself with a courtliness harking back to the days of
the New Deal liberalism that he espouses to a greater extent
than any of his rivals. An Illinois congressman from 1975 to
1984, then elected a senator, he started in national politics
comparatively late, having been a newspaper owner and
editor and a local politician in the small town of Troy. He was
the son of a Lutheran pastor and at the age of nineteen he had
bought the weekly *Troy Tribune*, with a circulation of less
than 2,000, and turned it into a campaigning newspaper
exposing local corruption. He has written eleven books.

  In the Senate he sits on two important committees, foreign
relations and the budget. His programme was the most
consistently liberal of any candidate's. In foreign affairs he
opposed the development of Star Wars and wanted to see an
end to US aid to the Contras. He wanted to spend more on
welfare (although recipients would have to work if they
could), on higher salaries for teachers and on creating new
jobs. He would increase taxes for people earning more than
$100,000 a year and levy a tax on oil imports. Questions were

raised in the press as to whether this package would result in a balanced budget, as he claimed.

Starting the campaign with a recognition factor close to zero, Simon soldiered on doggedly until at the end of year he was just leading the field in Iowa, with Dukakis a close second; that was before Hart re-entered the race and temporarily took support from both. People seemed to feel more comfortable with the homespun Simon than with the more glossily packaged candidates. Like other lesser-known contenders from the north, he needed a strong showing in Iowa and/or New Hampshire to set his campaign alight, because he seemed unlikely to be among the leaders on Super Tuesday in the south. He was a good second in Iowa to Gephardt and a respectable third in New Hampshire, but the consensus was that he needed more than that to have any realistic prospects. He was a poor fourth in Minnesota and South Dakota and, short of money, said he would largely ignore Super Tuesday and go all out for a good showing in his home state of Illinois. His victory there gave him 162 convention delegates, so he would exert some influence on the horse-trading, at least.

Non-runners

For the Democrats, this category could have as much significance as the candidates who have actually declared themselves. As 1987 drew to an end with no clearly electable front-runner, there was a growing call for a white knight of national stature to appear from elsewhere and ride off with the nomination.

Bill Bradley, a former professional basket-ball player (New York Knickerbockers, 1967–77) and senator from New Jersey since 1979, has a solid reputation but an unexciting speaking style. On the face of it, an unlikely saviour, although he arranged a visit to Moscow for early in 1988 just in case his lack of foreign policy experience should ever become an issue. A poll of Democrats in December 1987 showed that thirty-one per cent wanted Bradley among the candidates, compared with forty-one per cent who wanted Mario Cuomo (see below). But shortly afterwards he declared he was not a candidate.

Bill Clinton, Governor of Arkansas from 1979–81, and again since 1983, declared his non-candidacy at a press conference in July, 1987, at which he had been expected to announce his entry into the contest. His departure raised new speculation about the intentions of another powerful southerner, Senator Sam Nunn, but he also pulled out two months later (see below).

Mario Cuomo, Governor of New York state, declared in February 1987 that he would not be a candidate but that did not prevent speculation that he would be willing to come in as the party's saviour at the last moment. He never specifically ruled that out and indeed many of his trips and speeches in the pre-election period seemed aimed at strengthening his claim. Not since Hubert Humphrey in 1968 has anybody won the nomination without contesting the primaries (although Humphrey received a few write-in votes in most of them, totalling just over two per cent). If one candidate were to arrive at the Atlanta convention with more than half the delegates committed to him, then under the rules he could not be defeated. But in the crowded field of 1988, there seemed little likelihood of that happening. A deadlock would leave the way clear for anyone who could secure majority backing, whether they had taken part in the primaries or not. Alternatively, if the early primaries and caucuses had proved inconclusive, Cuomo could enter in later contests in some of the larger states, including California.

An Italian-American Catholic aged fifty-six, the son of an immigrant grocer, Cuomo spent time practising and teaching law before entering state politics in the 1970s. He was Secretary of State in Albany from 1975–8, then, after an unsuccessful run for Mayor of New York city, became lieutenant-governor of the state, until elected governor in 1982, succeeding Hugh Carey. His national stature grew and was reinforced by his keynote speech at the 1984 convention in San Francisco.

One rumour during 1987 was that Cuomo, married with five children, would not run because of embarrassing personal or financial allegations against himself or his family that might come to the surface if he were a candidate. In fact, he was investigated by the press as if he *were* a candidate, and nothing suspect was uncovered. His campaign consultant David Garth advised him to stay on the sidelines for tactical reasons. 'Cuomo should never go to the dance,' he said. 'He won't be in demand if he does.'

While avoiding the dance he was making statesmanlike gestures, such as arranging a meeting with Vice-President Bush to put forward his plan for a National Economic Commission to tackle poverty, and going to Moscow, where he made speeches about detente, arms control and human rights – an issue that Jewish and other ethnic voters take very seriously. It was his first visit to an Eastern bloc country. He intensified his schedule of public speeches outside his home state, making an average of one such appearance every two weeks during 1987.

Other candidates resented his undeclared campaign. 'If I get beaten I want it to be by someone who is playing on the field,' said Jesse Jackson. But senior figures in the party, appalled by the lack of quality among the declared runners, publicly urged Cuomo to place his name on the list. A poll for *Time* in December 1987 found that forty-one per cent of Democrats wanted him to do so. He conceded to the extent of saying he would accept the nomination as an obligation if the party thought there was no alternative figure with any prospect of winning. Even if he did sit it out, he would exert a powerful influence on the selection and could himself be a strong candidate for 1992.

During the campaign for the New York primary on 21 April, Cuomo received as much press coverage as the actual candidates. Although he made several statements deterring speculation about his nomination, he declined to say unambiguously that he would not accept it, and he did not give his formal endorsement to anybody. Instead, he praised each of the three remaining contenders – Dukakis, Jackson and Gore

– in turn. It was apparent that speculation about his possible candidacy would not finally die until the Atlanta convention had made the selection official.

Edward Kennedy, senator from Massachusetts, younger brother both of an assassinated President and an assassinated presidential candidate, seems to have made a career out of not quite being a presidential candidate himself. The closest he came was in 1980, when he challenged the incumbent President Carter for the nomination (see page 69). But he never truly escaped from the shadow of the Chappaquiddick accident. He declared categorically in December 1985 that he would not be a candidate in 1988 and nobody made any serious effort to persuade him to change his mind.

Sam Nunn would have commanded a big following in the south had he run, probably destroying the chance of Albert Gore. Although only forty-nine, he is one of the most experienced and respected southerners in Congress, having been a senator for Georgia since 1973, with four years service in the House of Representatives before that. Nunn, chairman of the Senate armed services committee, is an expert on defence and one of the minority of Democrats who support the deployment of the Strategic Defence Initiative (Star Wars). He probably calculated that he had many years left to make a presidential bid and that this was not the year for it. He announced his non-participation in the race in August 1987, but many were seeking to persuade him to change his mind if Cuomo persisted in his refusal to be drafted. In the run-up to the convention he became increasingly mentioned as a possible vice-presidential candidate if Dukakis won the nomination. As such, he would attract Southern votes to the ticket.

Charles Robb, former Governor of Virginia and son-in-law of the late President Johnson, was briefly touted as an alternative southerner in the wake of Nunn's withdrawal but showed no inclination to make the race.

Patricia Schroeder almost qualifies for 'dropout' status, for although she never declared herself a candidate she was regarded as a sure enough runner in the summer of 1987 to inspire her characterisation as Snow White to the Democrats'

Seven Dwarfs. She travelled up and down the country preparing the way for a campaign but at the end of September 1987, with the press widely anticipating the declaration of her candidacy, she announced tearfully that she had decided it was too late for her to begin organising. 'I'd love to be running but I haven't figured it out yet,' she sobbed.

Schroeder would have added some colour to the campaign, for she has a reputation for being outspoken on issues as broad-ranging as defence, the environment and feminism. She was the first woman to serve on the House armed services committee. Aged forty-seven, married with two children, she has been an energetic member of Congress from Colorado for fifteen years. She is popular with the press, chiefly for having invented the term the 'Teflon President' for Ronald Reagan. (Teflon is a surface to which nothing sticks.) Like some of the other non-combatants this year, she may have her eyes on future campaigns for the White House.

The Primaries

The primary system seems odd to countries that do not have it and are accustomed to playing out their candidate selection procedures in the relative privacy of their internal party mechanisms. One difficulty with the American way is that candidates spend many months attacking each other in the most forceful terms and are then supposed to undergo a miraculous transformation at convention time, rallying behind the winner. Voters' memories are notoriously short but not *that* short and if a candidate denounces his opponent as a wimp in June, it is unconvincing if he declares in August that he is the best qualified person to occupy the White House. Jimmy Carter's losing campaign in 1980 was thought to have suffered particularly from his primary battles with Edward Kennedy.

The Republicans in 1988 recognised that danger early on and tried to organise a non-aggression pact, but it did not last long. Dole's strategists argued that, as Vice-President, Bush had the advantage of a high public profile – an advantage he was not slow to exploit on occasions such as Mikhail Gorbachev's visit to Washington. To counteract this, they believed that Dole, easily the closest challenger, had no alternative but to attack Bush's personality and record: not to do so would make the televised debates even duller than they were.

There was less venom in the early stages of the Democratic contest because, with no clear front runner, candidates feared that to direct their fire on any particular rival would give the intended victim undue prominence and would thus be counter-productive. But there were so many televised debates that they had to show a bit of aggression to avoid increasing the boredom factor among long-suffering viewers. As soon as the polls showed a clear shift towards one contender, the others would regard him as fair game and get him in their sights.

Most candidates made their formal declarations of entering the race (or in some cases of not entering it) between the spring and autumn of 1987, but many had been campaigning since before that. By the end of the year the press and television news organisations had formed their campaign teams and reports began appearing in the newspapers carrying datelines of obscure communities in Iowa and New Hampshire, enjoying their quadrennial moment of national fame. Farmers, petrol pump attendants and waitresses were milked for insights into the workings of the mid-western and New England rural mind, and duly produced pearls of homespun wisdom. Candidates were scrutinised in detailed profiles when they entered the race and again when, like Gephardt, they seemed to be making an impact in the first caucus and primary states. The numerous television debates were earnestly analysed for gaffes, for new policy departures by one or other of the candidates, and for signs that any one of them might be gaining an advantage over the others. After a while, commentators complained that the debates were becoming tedious – and that was before any of the primaries had taken place.

The start of the presidential campaign year in January is marked by a lugubrious ritual. The secret service assigns special agents to candidates who believe they need protection. Some who do not feel especially threatened prefer to do without it at the primary stage, because the presence of security guards discourages direct contact between candidates and voters.

Many millions of dollars are spent in the months leading up to the opening of the primary season. In February the Federal Election Commission, which supervises campaign spending to see that the rules are not being broken (see page 88), released the following figures for each candidate's revenue (including federal matching funds) and spending up to the eve of the Iowa caucuses. They showed that some candidates were getting near the $27.6m limit of expenditure in the primaries. The figures are rounded to the nearest million dollars and candidates who withdrew before Super Tuesday have been omitted:

	Raised	*Spent*
Republicans		
Robertson	$28m	$22m
Bush	$27m	$15m
Dole	$21m	$16m
Kemp	$16m	$15m
Democrats		
Dukakis	$16m	$12m
Gephardt	$7m	$6m
Simon	$6m	$5m
Gore	$5m	$3m
Hart	$3m	$2m
Jackson	$2m	$1m

In the Democratic contest, the opinion polls in both Iowa and New Hampshire had been volatile in the weeks leading to the actual voting. Gary Hart's re-entry was the main cause of the fluctuations but by the end of January his fortunes were waning. Dukakis regained the lead in New Hampshire and Gephardt looked like beating both Simon and Hart, the earlier leaders, in Iowa. For the Republicans, Dole was favourite in Iowa and Bush in New Hampshire. Bush was also hoping to do better than his main opponent in the south on Super Tuesday, although Robertson was an unknown factor here. Of the Democrats, Jackson was likely to do best in the south, with its comparatively high proportion of black voters.

But before these main events came a sideshow in the form of the Republican delegate selection convention in Michigan, where the first seventy-seven delegates would be chosen for the Republican convention in New Orleans. This was a new event on the political calendar and, as it turned out, a confusing and rancorous one. Because it would be the first test of strength of the year, supporters of Pat Robertson had teamed up with those of Jack Kemp in an attempt to gain control of the state party and thus be in a strong position to nominate a majority of delegates.

Supporters of George Bush hit back and took legal action to prevent the take-over. The result was that when the state convention was held in Grand Rapids at the end of January, there were disputes between rival sets of delegates as to which had the right to represent their districts. The Bush faction – now supported by backers of Kemp, who had switched sides – came out on top. They chose thirty-seven Bush delegates, thirty-two for Kemp and eight for Robertson. (Dole, perhaps wisely, had stayed clear of the whole proceeding.) But the Robertson people held an alternative convention and chose forty-three for Robertson, twenty-one for Kemp and thirteen for Bush, thus ensuring an old-style credentials battle (see page 75) over the Michigan delegation at New Orleans.

The Iowa caucuses were preceded by the usual photographs and descriptive prose of snow scenes. Then came the detailed 'colour' reports of what actually happened at the caucuses, as crowds of party loyalists gathered in school rooms and even private homes to mull over their choices. After the build-up, it was a relief to have some real results, rather than opinion polls, for the experts to analyse. When they did, they agreed that on the Republican side Dole and Robertson had emerged surprisingly strongly and that Bush appeared to be fading. The Vice-President's political obituaries were already being written, alongside essays about the moral and religious dimension to Republican politics. The Democratic result had been closer to the predictions, with Gephardt confirmed as the front runner and Simon, four points behind him, judged not to have done quite well enough to stay seriously in the reckoning.

It was the Republicans again who stole the limelight in New Hampshire. This time it was Bush's turn to do better than expected and the experts had to revise their predictions quickly. Dole was nine per cent behind Bush: a bigger gap than the last opinion polls had predicted. As the British Prime Minister Harold Wilson said in another context, a week is a long time in politics. Now it was Bush with the momentum and Dole with the question-marks. Dole reacted sourly, snapping abuse at his rival, confirming his reputation for a malevolent disposition. Robertson's performance – a ten per cent share – had been disappointing after Iowa, but he was expected to show his strength in the south.

The Democratic contest in New Hampshire went much as expected. Dukakis's winning margin of seventeen per cent over Gephardt would have been impressive had it not been so widely anticipated. By coming second, Gephardt confirmed his position among the front runners. Paul Simon's third place again did not seem good enough and Hart was attracting virtually no support.

After New Hampshire the Republican field had dwindled by two, with the loss of Haig and du Pont. For the Democrats, only Babbitt had so far dropped out. The dwindling circus moved south for Super Tuesday, some candidates making isolated forays back into the snowbelt for the relatively insignificant contests in Minnesota and South Dakota. Dole, whose territory this was, won both. This had been expected and Bush had limited his campaigning in the two states, preferring to concentrate on the southern contests two weeks later. The results did, however, have the effect of restoring some of the momentum Dole had lost in New Hampshire. On the Democratic side the frontrunners Dukakis and Gephardt fought an honourable draw, with Dukakis winning in Minnesota and Gephardt in South Dakota.

A week later the Maine caucuses restored Bush's fortunes by giving him a clean sweep of the twenty-two Republican delegates, while Dukakis, again on his New England home ground, led the Democrats, with Jesse Jackson coming second and showing once more that he could attract non-black votes. Opinion polls indicated that Bush and Dukakis were also likely to do well on Super Tuesday. The other Republicans, sensing that Bush was taking an unassailable lead, began to gang up on him in the televised debates, making ever more direct assaults on his record during the Reagan administration. Bush retaliated by declining to take part in any more debates before Super Tuesday – a stance that as the front runner he now felt justified in taking. In the South Carolina Republican primary, three days before Super Tuesday, Bush won by a much greater margin than had been predicted, gaining forty-eight per cent of the vote: more than twice as much as Dole. Robertson, in a state where he was expected to do well, could not rise above nineteen per cent. Kemp, with only twelve per cent, seemed certain to be the next to withdraw.

For the Democrats, Dukakis appeared to be shaping up the best, taking advantage of his facility in languages to be filmed for the TV news haranguing Texas migrant workers in Spanish. The fact that his home state of Massachusetts was among those with primaries on Super Tuesday meant that he was sure of at least one good win, and he was also expected to do well in the north-western state of Washington. Jesse Jackson, with a virtual stranglehold on the substantial black vote and with some white liberal support, looked likely to win the south overall, with Dukakis doing well enough to keep his front-runner status. Polls showed Gephardt to be losing ground and Gore, who was staking everything on a strong showing in the south, did not appear to be doing quite well enough. Hart and Simon, both desperately short of money, were effectively out of the race, although Simon was expected to keep his candidacy going until after the primary in Illinois, his home state, the following week.

The actual results on 8 March confirmed most of these predictions. Bush's victory margin was again greater than expected – fifty-six per cent, against twenty-four for Dole, thirteen for Robertson and five for Kemp, who withdrew two days later. It looked as though Bush, with seemingly unstoppable momentum, was now certain of the nomination. The Democrats had virtually a three-way tie: Jackson with twenty-seven per cent and Dukakis and Gore with twenty-six each, and Gephardt a bad fourth with thirteen. Gore was seen as the main beneficiary, because he had exceeded the pollsters' expectations. It now seemed certain that no candidate would go to the convention with a majority of the delegates, leaving all to play for in Atlanta and renewing speculation about the entry of Mario Cuomo or one of the other undeclared candidates.

For the Republicans, it was soon all over. Illinois was the kind of state that Dole, a mid-Westerner, would have had to win to sustain his candidacy, but Bush gained 56 per cent of the vote to Dole's 37. After another heavy defeat in Connecticut, Dole withdrew at the end of March and threw his weight behind the Vice-President. Only Pat Robertson now remained formally in contention with Bush, but had curtailed his campaign, seemingly content with the handful of delegates he would take to New Orleans to try to exert some moral influence on the platform and perhaps secure a foothold for the future.

The Republicans were now presenting an effectively united party to the electorate. While this might be of long-term benefit, the immediate effect was that the press concentrated on the still undecided Democratic race. Bush made some campaign appearances in New York to keep his face fleetingly before the cameras, but all the headlines were devoted to Dukakis, Jackson and Gore as they campaigned in the city's varied ethnic neighbourhoods.

Of the trio, Jackson commanded the most attention after

finishing ahead of Dukakis in both Illinois and Michigan. It was now apparent that, unlike in 1984, Jackson was appealing to both white and black liberal voters – something that the experts had not foreseen, despite his strong showing in the opinion polls in the run-up to the primaries. In a wave of self-criticism, commentators decided that they had been guilty of underestimating his chance of actually winning the nomination. The media made up for it with long profiles and interviews. News magazines printed his picture on the front cover. Leaders of the Democratic Party, who had shared the presumption that he could not be nominated, were now greatly dismayed, for they believed that to choose a black candidate would be a certain way of losing the election in November.

The result in Wisconsin eased their worries, for Jackson did less well there than the opinion polls had predicted. Dukakis was now safely back in the lead. He beat Jackson by 14 per cent in New York and, short of an unanticipated disaster in the later primaries, seemed sure to go to Atlanta with the majority of committed delegates. Moreover, opinion polls showed that Dukakis would have a good chance of beating Bush in the election. With six months to go before the Tuesday that really mattered, the two sides had moved close to selecting their standard-bearers.

After New York, the total number of candidates committed to each candidate was as follows:

REPUBLICANS (1139 needed for nomination)
Bush	1099
Robertson	17
Uncommitted	228

DEMOCRATS (2082 needed for nomination)
Dukakis	1029
Jackson	883
Gore	433
Simon	184
Uncommitted	617

1988 PRIMARIES AND CAUCUSES

			Republicans			*Democrats*		
			Dels	Form	Winner	Dels	Form	Winner
Jan	29/30	MICHIGAN	77	Con	Bush†	138	OC	Jackson
Feb	8	IOWA	37	OC	Dole	52	OC	Gephardt
	16	NEW HAMPSHIRE	23	OP	Bush	18	OP	Dukakis
	23	MINNESOTA	31	OC	Dole	78	OC	Dukakis
	23	SOUTH DAKOTA	18	CP	Dole	15	CP	Gephardt
	26–28	MAINE	22	OC	Bush	23	OC	Dukakis
Mar	1	ALASKA	19	CC	–	12	CC	Jackson
Mar	5	SOUTH CAROLINA	37	OP	Bush	44	OC	Jackson
	8	ALABAMA	38	OP	Bush	56	OP	Jackson
	8	ARKANSAS	27	OP	Bush	38	OP	Gore
	8	FLORIDA	82	CP	Bush	136	CP	Dukakis
	8	GEORGIA	48	OP	Bush	77	OP	Jackson
	8	HAWAII	20	CC	–	20	CC	Dukakis
	8	IDAHO	22	OP	(on May 24)	18	OC	Dukakis
	8	KENTUCKY	38	CP	Bush	55	CP	Gore
	8	LOUISIANA	41	CP	Bush	63	CP	Jackson
	8	MARYLAND	41	CP	Bush	67	CP	Dukakis
	8	MASSACHUSETTS	52	OP	Bush	98	OP	Dukakis
	8	MISSISSIPPI	31	OP	Bush	40	OP	Jackson
	8	MISSOURI	47	OP	Bush	77	OP	Gephardt
	8	NEVADA	20	CC	–	16	CC	Gore
	8	NORTH CAROLINA	54	CP	Bush	82	CP	Gore
	8	OKLAHOMA	36	CP	Bush	46	CP	Gore
	8	RHODE ISLAND	21	OP	Bush	22	OP	Dukakis
	8	TENNESSEE	45	OP	Bush	70	OP	Gore
	8	TEXAS	111	OP	Bush	183	OP	Dukakis
	8	VIRGINIA	50	OC	Bush	75	OP	Jackson
	8	WASHINGTON	41	OC	Robertson	65	OC	Dukakis
	13–27	NORTH DAKOTA	16	OP	(on June 14)	15	OC	Dukakis
	15	ILLINOIS	92	OP	Bush	173	OP	Simon
	20	PUERTO RICO	14	OP	Bush	51	OP	Jackson
	22	DEMS ABROAD			–	7	OP	Dukakis
	29	CONNECTICUT	35	CP	Bush	52	CP	Dukakis
Apl	1–30	DELAWARE	17	CC	–	15	CC	Jackson
	2	VIRGIN ISLANDS	4	CC	–	3	CC	Jackson
	4	COLORADO	36	CC	Bush	45	CC	Dukakis
	5	WISCONSIN	47	OP	Bush	81	OP	Dukakis
	16	ARIZONA	33	CC	(on Apl 24)	36	CC	Dukakis
	19	NEW YORK	136	CP	Bush	255	CP	Dukakis
	19	VERMONT	17	OC	Bush	14	OC	Dukakis
	25	UTAH	26	OC	Bush	23	OC	Dukakis

		State	Republicans			Democrats		
			Dels	Form	Winner	Dels	Form	Winner
	26	PENNSYLVANIA	96	CP	Bush	178	CP	Dukakis
May	3	DC	14	CP	Bush	16	CP	Jackson
	3	INDIANA	51	OP	Bush	79	OP	Dukakis
	3	OHIO	88	OP	Bush	159	OP	Dukakis
	10	NEBRASKA	25	CP		25	CP	
	10	WEST VIRGINIA	28	OP		37	OP	
	17	OREGON	32	CP		45	CP	
June	7	CALIFORNIA	175	CP		314	CP	
	7	MONTANA	20	OP		19	OP	
	7	NEW JERSEY	64	OP		109	OP	
	7	NEW MEXICO	26	CP		24	CP	

CC = closed caucus, CP = closed primary, OC = open caucus, OP = open primary,
Con. = convention. *Vermont and Virginia Republicans also had non-binding primaries.
†The Michigan result was disputed by supporters of Pat Robertson.

STATE-BY-STATE GUIDE TO CONGRESSIONAL REPRESENTATION FOLLOWING 1986 ELECTIONS

State	US Senate		US House of Reps		State Governor
	D	R	D	R	
Alabama	2	–	5	2	R
Alaska	–	2	–	1	D
Arizona	1	1	1	4	R
Arkansas	2	–	3	1	D
California	1	1	27	18	R
Colorado	1	1	3	3	D
Connecticut	1	1	3	3	D
Delaware	1	1	1	1	R
Florida	2	–	12	7	R
Georgia	2	–	8	2	D
Hawaii	2	–	1	1	D
Idaho	–	2	1	1	D
Illinois	2	–	13	9	R
Indiana	–	2	6	4	R
Iowa	1	1	2	4	R
Kansas	–	2	2	3	R

State	US Senate		US House of Reps		State Governor
	D	R	D	R	
Kentucky	1	1	4	3	D
Louisiana	2	–	5	3	D
Maine	1	1	1	1	R
Maryland	2	–	6	2	D
Massachusetts	2	–	10	1	D
Michigan	2	–	11	7	D
Minnesota	–	2	5	3	D
Mississippi	1	1	4	1	D
Missouri	–	2	5	4	R
Montana	2	–	1	1	D
Nebraska	2	–	–	3	R
Nevada	1	1	1	1	D
New Hampshire	–	2	–	2	R
New Jersey	2	–	8	6	R
New Mexico	1	1	1	2	D
New York	1	1	20	14	D
North Carolina	1	1	8	3	R
North Dakota	2	–	1	–	D
Ohio	2	–	11	10	D
Oklahoma	1	1	4	2	R
Oregon	–	2	3	2	D
Pennsylvania	–	2	12	11	D
Rhode Island	1	1	1	1	R
South Carolina	1	1	4	2	R
South Dakota	1	1	1	–	R
Tennessee	2	–	6	3	D
Texas	1	1	17	10	R
Utah	–	2	1	2	R
Vermont	1	1	–	1	D
Virginia	–	2	5	5	D
Washington	1	1	5	3	D
West Virginia	2	–	4	–	R
Wisconsin	1	1	5	4	R
Wyoming	1	1	–	1	D

8

Other 1988 Contests

Congress

Against the dramatic backdrop of a presidential election, the significance of the other contests under way on election night could be overlooked, particularly by viewers overseas. Yet even if control of the House of Representatives is unlikely to change – the Democratic majority of seventy-eight in a 435-seat House looks safe enough – there is an outside chance that the Republicans could capture the Senate, where the Democratic majority is only eight. To have the House and the Senate controlled by different parties does not make life especially easy for a new President, although it gives him a pretext for asserting his own authority over a warring Congress. It is certainly preferable to having both chambers dominated by political opponents, as President Reagan has had to endure during the last two years of his term. They can frustrate the Presidential will in matters such as appointments and foreign aid. A hostile Congress was the prime cause of the debacle over Reagan's Supreme Court nominees, and of thwarting the President's desire to send new aid to the Contra rebels in Nicaragua.

Of the thirty-three Senate seats being contested this year (listed on page 199), the Democrats hold eighteen and the Republicans fifteen. To wipe out the Democratic majority in the upper house the Republicans need capture only four of their opponents' seats, assuming that they hold on to all those they are themselves defending. If that happened, the President, whoever he is, would effectively control the Senate through the casting vote of the Vice-President in the event of deadlock. A strong showing by the Republican presidential candidate could conceivably create enough of a 'coat-tails' effect to allow the vital four seats to change hands, but the odds are against it.

The presidential campaign certainly has a strong influence on the congressional contests. 1988 is, after all, the one year in four when Americans are exposed to politics at saturation level. If, come November, they are not aware of the issues and philosophies that divide the parties and their candidates, they are never going to be. Turnout for elections in a presidential year is usually about twenty per cent higher than in years when only members of Congress are being elected – although at only fifty-three per cent in 1986, the turnout was still low.

This year, Republican candidates will have been harmed by the Iran-Contra scandal, reviving memories of Watergate, as well as by the economic problems of Reagan's last two years and his apparent indecision about how to handle them. Balancing that, however, the Democrats will suffer from the long drawn-out pre-primary campaign, the image of their most likely contenders as the 'seven dwarfs', and the consequent appearance of a lack of direction and leadership in the party.

The thirty-three Senate seats were last contested six years ago, so theoretically there is a greater chance of a swing to one party or another than in the House of Representatives, all of whose members were elected in 1986. There is a further factor that makes Senate races hard to predict: serving six-year terms, senators build up a strong personal following, regardless of party. This becomes a greater factor the longer they serve – and some go on until they are past eighty, racking up larger majorities every six years. Thus it is not necessarily the case, as it usually is in Britain, that the narrower the majority the more likely the seat is to change hands. Voters are less likely to vote for a party label when electing a senator than when choosing other office-holders.

The contest to be a congressional candidate is altogether shorter than for the presidency. The primaries – separate

from the presidential ones – start in March but the last few are
not finalised until early October. So it is impossible to say
precisely who all the candidates will be until a few weeks
before the election. Earlier in the year, some glamorous
names were being canvassed. Colonel Oliver North, master-
mind of the Iran/Contra deals, was thinking of running in
Virginia (conveniently close to Washington DC). So were
Alexander Haig, the former Secretary of State and an early
dropout from the presidential race, and Pat Robertson, the
television evangelist, assuming *his* presidential ambitions
would not be fulfilled.

Of senators running for re-election, Edward Kennedy is the
best known. He is virtually certain of re-election in Massachusetts, despite his public dispute early in 1988 with
Rupert Murdoch, the international press tycoon who numbers the *Boston Herald* in his stable of newspapers. (Kennedy
was trying to force Murdoch to comply with the rules of the
Federal Communications Commission that bar owning a
newspaper and a television station in the same city.) Robert
Byrd of West Virginia is another national figure seeking a new
six-year term – in his case his sixth. Daniel Moynihan, the
outspoken Democratic senator from New York, faced a
potential Republican challenge from Rudolph Giuliani, the
Manhattan district attorney, or Ronald Lauder, from the
Estee Lauder perfume dynasty.

John Stennis, the 86-year-old veteran who has represented
Mississippi since 1947, was leaving people guessing until the
last minute whether or not he would seek re-election. The
most notable of those retiring is Senator William Proxmire of
Wisconsin, a redoubtable campaigner against waste by the
federal government.

Below is a list of the Senate seats being contested this year.
Those senators marked with an asterisk have publicly
announced their intention to stand down. Others, however,
still have to be selected by their parties as candidates, and a
few may not be. In the ratings column on the far right, V is for
vulnerable, HV highly vulnerable, PV potentially vulnerable
and PS probably safe, based on local factors as calculated by

the *Congressional Quarterly*. A table showing the present membership of the House of Representatives is on page 194.

	Incumbent (*=retiring this year)	Party	Previous vote (%)	Rating (see above)
ARIZONA	Dennis DeConcini	D	57	PS
CALIFORNIA	Pete Wilson	R	52	PV
CONNECTICUT	Lowell Weicker Jr	R	50	PV
DELAWARE	William Roth Jr	R	55	PV
FLORIDA	Lawton Chiles	D	62	V
HAWAII	Spark Matsunaga	D	80	PS
INDIANA	Richard Lugar	R	54	PS
MAINE	George Mitchell	D	61	PS
MARYLAND	Paul Sarbanes	D	64	PS
MASSACHUSETTS	Edward Kennedy	D	61	PS
MICHIGAN	Donald Riegle Jr	D	58	PS
MINNESOTA	Dave Durenberger	R	53	V
MISSISSIPPI	John Stennis	D	64	PV
MISSOURI	John Danforth	R	51	PS
MONTANA	John Melcher	D	55	PV
NEBRASKA	David Karnes	R	apptd. 1987	HV
NEVADA	Chic Hecht	R	50	HV
NEW JERSEY	Frank Lautenberg	D	51	V
NEW MEXICO	Jeff Bingaman	D	54	PV
NEW YORK	Daniel Moynihan	D	65	PV
NORTH DAKOTA	Quentin Burdick	D	63	PS
OHIO	Howard Metzenbaum	D	57	V
PENNSYLVANIA	John Heinz	R	59	PS
RHODE ISLAND	John Chafee	R	51	V
TENNESSEE	Jim Sasser	D	62	PS
TEXAS	Lloyd Bentsen	D	59	PS
UTAH	Orrin Hatch	R	58	PS
VERMONT	Robert Stafford*	R		PS
VIRGINIA	Paul Trible Jr*	R		V
WASHINGTON	Daniel Evans	R	55	PV
WEST VIRGINIA	Robert Byrd	D	69	PS
WISCONSIN	William Proxmire*	D		V
WYOMING	Malcolm Wallop	R	57	PS

Governors' races

Twelve state governorships are also to be filled this year. Nine of them were last contested in 1984, the year of the Reagan landslide. (Vermont, Rhode Island and New Hampshire elect their governors every two years.) Like senators, governors are chosen to a large extent for the personal qualities they project to the electorate. Where matters of policy impinge they are more likely to be on the parochial than on the national level. All the same, Reagan's copious coat-tails appeared to have an effect four years ago and only four of the governors' results then bucked the Republican trend – Montana, North Dakota, Vermont and Washington. This means that the Republicans are defending in eight of the twelve contests, so any gains for them this year would be against the mathematical odds. Democrats sit in twenty-six of the country's fifty governors' mansions – a bare majority, but the figure has no significance except as an (unreliable) indicator of the national political mood. With only four Democratic governorships as targets this year, it seems unlikely that the Republicans will be able to reduce that slender Democratic lead. These are the states with contests for governor this year:

	Incumbent	Party	Last vote (%) and year
DELAWARE	Michael Castle	R	55 (1984)
INDIANA	Robert Orr	R	53 (1984)
MISSOURI	John Ashcroft	R	57 (1984)
MONTANA	Ted Schwinden	D	73 (1984)
NEW HAMPSHIRE	John Sununu	R	54 (1986)
NORTH CAROLINA	James Martin	R	54 (1984)
NORTH DAKOTA	George Sinner	D	55 (1984)
RHODE ISLAND	Edward DiPrete	R	67 (1986)
UTAH	Norman Bangerter	R	56 (1984)
VERMONT	Madeleine Kunin	D	47* (1986)
WASHINGTON	Booth Gardner	D	53 (1984)
WEST VIRGINIA	Arch Moore Jr,	R	53 (1984)

*=in three-cornered contest.

SOURCES

There are thousands of books about United States politics and the presidency. Below is a list of those to which I referred in writing this one. For the chapters about the 1988 contest I drew on contemporary reportage in the *Congressional Quarterly*, *National Journal*, *Time* and *Newsweek* in Washington and, in London, *The Independent*, *The Guardian*, *The Times*, *The Observer*, *The Economist*, *The Sunday Times*, *Sunday Telegraph* and *International Herald Tribune*. I also used the reference library at the United States Information Service in London and I am grateful for the enthusiastic help of the staff there.

The books listed below are published in London except where stated:

ADAMS, Dr William C.: *As New Hampshire Goes . . .* (Essay in collection listed below under ORREN.)

ARMBRUSTER, Maxim E.: *The Presidents of the United States*. Horizon, New York, 1966.

BENDINER, Robert: *White House Fever*. Methuen, 1960.

BRAMS, Steven J.: *The Presidential Election Game*. Yale University Press, 1978.

BROGAN, D. W.: *An Introduction to American Politics*. Hamish Hamilton, 1954.

CARTER, Jimmy: *Keeping Faith*. Collins, 1982.

COOKE, Alistair: *The Americans*. Knopf, New York, 1979.

The Constitution of the United States and the Declaration of Independence. Doubleday, Garden City.

CORWIN, Edward S.: *The President*. New York University Press, 1984.

DENENBERG, R. V.: *Understanding American Politics*. Fontana, 1976.

ECONOMIST INTELLIGENCE UNIT: *The World in 1988*. Economist Publications, 1987.

ESTALL, Robert: *A Modern Geography of the United States*. Penguin, 1976.

FAWCETT, Edmund, and THOMAS, Tony: *America, Americans*. Collins, 1983.

FORD, Gerald R.: *A Time to Heal*. W. H. Allen, 1979.

GARREAU, Joel: *The Nine Nations of North America*. Houghton Mifflin, Boston, 1977.

GOLDINGER, Carolyn (ed.): *Presidential Elections Since 1789*. Congressional Quarterly, Washington, 1987.

GRAY, Lee Learner: *How We Choose a President*. St James Press, 1976.

HODGSON, Godfrey: *All Things to All Men*. Penguin, 1984.

JAMIESON, Kathleen Hall: *Packaging the Presidency*. Oxford University Press, 1984.

LARSON, Arthur: *Eisenhower: the President Nobody Knew*. Leslie Frewin, 1969.

LEISH, Kenneth W.: *The White House*. Newsweek, New York, 1972.

MANCHESTER, William: *The Glory and the Dream*. Michael Joseph, 1975.

NATIONAL SECURITY ARCHIVE: *The Chronology*. Warner, New York, 1987.

ORREN, Gary R. and POLSBY, Nelson W. (eds): *Media and Momentum: The New Hampshire Primary and Nomination Politics*. Chatham House Publishers, Chatham, NJ, 1987.

POLSBY, Nelson W. and WILDAVSKY, Aaron: *Presidential Elections*. Charles Scribner's Sons, New York, 1984.

ROSEBOOM, Eugene H. and ECKES, Alfred E. Jr: *A History of Presidential Elections*. Collier Macmillan, 1979.

ROSSITER, Clinton: *Parties and Politics in America*. Signet, New York, 1960.

SCHROEDER, Richard S.: *An Outline of American Government*. United States Information Agency, Washington, 1980.

SHAW, Malcolm (ed.): *The Modern Presidency*. Harper and Row, New York, 1987.

WHITE, Theodore H.: *America in Search of Itself*. Harper and Row, New York, 1982.

World Book Encyclopaedia. World Book Inc., Chicago, 1985.

Index

Adams, Abigail 105
Adams, John 18, 105
Adams, John Quincy 19, 20
Adams, Sherman 48
Adams, William 78
Afghanistan 69
African National Congress 176
Agnew, Spiro 58, 59, 62, 163, 168
Agriculture, Department of 133
AIDS 147
Alabama 52, 115–17
Alaska 120–1
Anderson, John 99
Angola 64
Arab–Israeli War 67–8
Arizona 118–19, 173–4
Arkansas 124–5, 182
Arthur, Chester 30
Anti-Masonic Party 21–2
Articles of Confederation and
        Perpetual Union 12–13
Assassinations 25, 30, 34, 53

Babbitt, Bruce 143, 144, 173–4, 180
Baker, Howard 168
Bakker, Jim 148
Ballot 100–3
Bank of the United States 17
Bay of Pigs 51
Beecher, Rev. Henry Ward 93
Begin, Menachim 68
Berlin Wall 51
Biden, Joseph 93, 169, 174–5
Bill of Rights 129
'Black Monday' 142–3
Black Muslims 55
Black Panthers 55
Blaine, James 29, 30–1
Bogart, Humphrey 162
Bork, Robert 175
Boston Globe 158
Bradley, Bill 181–2
Breakfast Time 102
Brezhnev, Leonid 60, 64

Bristow, Benjamin 30
Broder, David 155, 157
Brown, Jerry 85
Bryan, William Jennings 32, 33, 90
Buchanan, James 24–5, 85
Buchanan, Patrick 168
Budget deficit 142–6
Bundy, McGeorge 134
van Buren, Martin 22
Burr, Aaron 18, 19
Bush, George 144, 149, 152, 153–62,
        163, 165–67, 183, 185–9, 191, 192
Byrd, Robert 198

California 78, 100, 118–19
Cambodia 59
Camelot 50, 54
Camp David 68, 106
Campaigning 83–4, 87–9
Capitol 104, 105
Carey, Hugh 182
Carter, James E. 65, 67–70, 71, 79, 80,
        83, 85, 92, 94, 95, 97, 102–3, 103,
        111, 113, 115, 117, 119–21, 125,
        131, 147, 161, 163, 173, 174, 176,
        184, 185
Carter, Lillian 66
Carter, Rosalynn 66, 85
Carter, Ruth 66
Castro, Fidel 51, 117
Caucuses 79–80, 82
Centralism 13
Chamoun, President 48
Chappaquiddick 70, 92, 184
'Checkers' speech (Nixon) 45, 91–2
Chiang Kai-Shek 44
Chicago convention (1968), 77
China 44, 60, 64
Chou En-lai 60
Christian Broadcasting Network (CBN)
        159–60
Churchill, Winston S. 40
CIA 51, 156
Civil Rights Act 52, 54, 56

Civil War 21, 24–6, 27, 28, 31, 74
Clay, Henry 23, 24
Cleveland, Grover 30–2, 93, 103
Clinton, Bill 182
Clinton, George 18
Colorado 120–1, 170, 185
Cold War 44
Commerce, Department of 132
Committee to Re-Elect the President (CREEP) 87
Confederacy 24–6
Congress 12, 13, 15, 21, 26, 28, 31, 35, 36, 38, 40, 42, 43, 44, 46, 47, 48, 39, 52, 54, 62, 64, 71, 104, 105, 126–31, 136, 138, 143, 153, 156
Connecticut 112–13, 170
Conservative Party (Britain) 22
Constitution 11–16, 23–4, 74, 126, 127, 128, 135, 138, 139
Contra aid 71, 72, 131, 150–2, 153, 156, 163, 167, 168
Conventions 96–8
Cooke, Alistair 62
Coolidge, Calvin 37
Cuba 33, 51–2, 117
Cuomo, Mario 83, 97, 170, 178, 182–4, 191

Darwin, Charles 34
Davis, John 37, 76
Deaver, Michael 148
Debs, Eugene 32, 33
Defence 148–50
Defense Department 132
Delaware 20, 113–15, 164
Democratic Party 17, 20, 22, 24, 26, 29, 30, 32, 33, 35–46, 49, 50, 52, 54, 57, 65, 70–74, 76, 77–80, 81, 83, 85, 87, 89–99, 110–112, 114, 121, · 127, 128, 143–7, 149, 150, 154, 158, 168–85, 186–95
Democratic Republicanism 17, 20
Department of Commerce census 109–10
Dewey, Thomas 39–40, 44, 87
Diem, Ngo Dinh 46
District of Columbia 61, 103, 105, 113–15, 127
'Dixiecrats' 43, 99, 111
Dole, Elizabeth 162–3

Dole, Robert 144, 149, 150, 152, 154, 155, 157–64, 166, 168, 185, 186, 187, 188, 189, 190, 191
Dred Scott decision 25
Dukakis, Kitty 170
Dukakis, Michael 152, 168–71, 173, 175, 176, 178, 181, 183, 184, 187–93
Dulles, John Foster 46

Eagleton, Thomas 61
East–West relations 148–50
Economy 142–6
Edison, Thomas 100
Education 146–7
Education, Department of 133, 147
Egypt 47, 68
Eisenhower, Dwight D. 45, 46–9, 76, 91, 94
Elections 12, 13, 15–16, 74–107
Electoral college 15–16
Electorate 109–25
Energy, Department of 133
Erlichman, John 134
Executive branch 131–5

Fall, Albert 37
Faubus, Orval 48
Fawcett, Edmund 115
Federal Bureau of Investigation (FBI) 132
Federal Elections Act (1974), 88
Federal government 126–41
Federalism 17, 18, 19, 23
Ferraro, Geraldine 158
Fillmore, Millard 24
First ladies 19, 36, 50, 85, 105–6
Fisk, Jim 28
Florida 29, 34, 75, 82, 115–17, 170
Ford, Gerald R. 62–66, 95, 113, 115, 117, 120, 121, 125, 155, 162, 163
Formosa 44
France 47
Franchise 15, 36, 74
Franklin, Benjamin 11–12
Fremont, John 24
Fund-raising 87–9

Garfield, James 30
Garth, David 83, 183

George III, 11
Georgia 66, 115–17, 184
Gephardt, Richard 145, 149, 152, 170,
	175–8, 181, 187–90, 193
Giuliani, Rudolph 198
Gold standard 32–3
Goldfine, Bernard 48
Goldwater, Barry 55, 111, 119, 155
Gorbachev, Mikhail 71, 149, 166, 186
Gore, Albert 149, 152, 170, 177–8, 183,
	184, 187, 190, 191–3
Gould, Jay 28
Grant, Gen. Ulysses S. 27–8, 30
Great Britain 11–13, 22, 47, 65
Great Compromise 13
'Great Society' (Johnson) 54
Guam 33, 75, 127
Gulf War 151–2

Haig, Alexander 165–6, 189, 198
Hamilton, Alexander 13, 15, 17, 18, 19
Harding, Warren 36–7
Harrison, Benjamin 32, 103
Harrison, William 22, 27, 32, 89
Hart, Gary 80, 81, 85, 92–3, 148, 154,
	174, 178–80, 187–90
Hart, Lee 178
Hawaii 120–1
Hayes, Rutherford 29
Health and Human Services,
	Department of 133
Hearst, William Randolph 33
Helsinki conference 64, 65
Hiroshima 42
Hispanics 112, 117
Ho Chi Minh 46
Hoban, James 105
Hollywood 45
Hoover, Herbert 37–8
House of Representatives 13, 16, 18,
	74, 103, 127–8, 129, 130
Housing Department 133
Humphrey, Hubert 57, 76, 78, 99, 119,
	182
Hungary 47

Idaho 120–1
Illinois 124–5, 173, 180
Impeachment 23–4, 26–7, 62, 129
Independence, War of 11–13

Indiana 113–15
INF agreement 149
Interior, Department of the 132
International Monetary Fund (IMF) 43,
	149
Iowa 78, 79, 124–5, 159, 161, 162, 167,
	170, 173, 174, 176, 177, 180, 181,
	187–8
Iran 68–9, 71–2, 131, 150–2, 153, 156,
	163, 167, 168
Israel 67–8

Jackson, Andrew 15, 19–20, 22, 23,
	27–8, 89
Jackson, Rev. Jesse 97, 144, 146–50,
	152, 156, 169–73, 183, 187, 188,
	190, 191–2, 193
Japan 39, 41
Jefferson, Thomas 17, 18
Jeffersonian Republicans 17
Jewish vote 114, 170
Johnson, Andrew 25–6, 27, 30
Johnson, Lyndon B. 53–8, 67, 74, 128,
	146, 184
Jordan, Hamilton 83
Judiciary 135–8, 139
Justice, Department of 132

Kansas 124–5, 161, 163, 179
Kemp, Jack 144, 145, 147, 149, 150,
	152, 157, 160, 164–7, 187, 188,
	190, 191
Kennedy, Edward 69, 70, 85, 92, 93,
	97, 184, 185, 198
Kennedy, Jacqueline 50, 106
Kennedy, John F. 49–53, 54, 58, 76, 85,
	88, 92, 94, 102, 103, 134, 175, 176
Kennedy, Joseph 49
Kennedy, Robert 50, 57
Kent State shootings 59
Khomeini, Ayatollah 68
Khrushchev, Nikita 51, 176
King, Martin Luther 52, 57, 171
King, Rufus 19
Kinnock, Neil 93, 169, 174, 175
Kirkpatrick, Jean 168
Kissinger, Henry 60, 61, 63, 134, 135
Koch, Ed 152, 178
Korean War 44–6
Kraft, Joseph 63

Labor Day 98
Labor Department 133
Labour Party (Britain) 93, 110, 169
Laffer, Arthur 145, 167
Lance, Bert 66–7, 172–3
Laos 60
Lauder, Ronald 198
Laxalt, Paul 168
League of Nations 43
Lebanon 48, 134
Lee, Gen. Robert E. 27
Lincoln, Abraham 25, 26, 30, 111
Literary Digest 36, 86
Little Rock 48
Louisiana 29, 115–17

MacArthur, Gen. Douglas 44
McCarthy, Eugene 57, 65–6, 76–7
McCarthy, Joseph 45, 47, 131
McGovern, George 61, 179
McKinley, William 32–3, 34
Madison, Dolley 19, 36, 105
Madison, James 19
Maine 112–13, 189
Mao Tse-tung 60
Marshall, John 136–7
Marshall Plan 43
Maryland 113–15
Massachusetts 61, 112–13, 168, 170,
    184, 190
Medicare 54
Meese, Edwin 148
Meredith, James 52
Mexico 118
Miami Herald 180
Michigan 113–15, 173, 188
Middle East conflict 47, 48, 63–4, 67,
    150–2
Minnesota 124–5, 176, 189
Mississippi 52, 115–17, 127
Missouri 124–5, 176
Mondale, Walter 71, 79, 81, 93–4, 113,
    115, 117, 120, 121, 124, 125, 162,
    178
Monroe, James 19, 20, 106
Monroe Doctrine 20
Montana 120–1
Montesquieu 12
Montgomery, Robert 49
Moral issues 147–8

Mormon church 121
Moscow Olympics, boycott of 69
Moynihan, Daniel 198
Mudd, Roger 92, 93
Murdoch, Rupert 198
Muskie, Edward 61
My Lai 59
MX missile 144

Nagasaki 42
Nasser, President 47
National Guard 139
National Rainbow Coalition 172
National Republican Party 22
National Security Commission 72, 134
National Union Party 25
NATO 43, 46
Nebraska 124–5
Nevada 120–1, 168
New Deal 38–40, 42, 54, 110
New England 19, 112–13, 159
New Hampshire 57, 76–7, 78, 82,
    112–13, 159, 161, 165–7, 169, 170,
    172–4, 176, 177, 180, 181, 187–8,
    189, 190
New Jersey 113–15, 181
New Mexico 118–19
New York 64, 78, 113–15, 166, 170,
    178, 182–3, 192
New York Times 60, 171
Nicaragua 71–2
Nixon, Patricia 106
Nixon, Richard 27, 45, 49, 57–64, 71,
    91–2, 99, 103, 131, 134–5, 138,
    155, 163, 165, 166, 168
Noriega, Gen. Manuel 151
North, Col. Oliver 72–3, 198
North Carolina 115–17, 164
North Dakota 124–5
Nunn, Sam 177, 182, 184

Observer 93
Office of Management and Budget 134
Ohio 113–15
Oklahoma 124–5
Opinion polls 86
Oregon 29, 120–1
Oswald, Lee Harvey 53
Oval office 104

Palestine Liberation Organisation (PLO) 67–8
Panama 151
Panama Canal 34, 67, 131
Party system 16–24
Patronage 20–1, 31–2
Peace Corps 50
Pearl Harbor 39
Pennsylvania 113–15
Pentagon Papers 60
Philadelphia Convention (1787), 11–15, 16
Philippines 33
Pinckney, C. C. 18, 19
Pinckney, Thomas 18
Poindexter, Admiral John 72, 156
Poland 94–5
Polk, James 24
du Pont, Pierre (Pete) 164–5, 189
Populist party 32
Presidential election 12, 13, 15–16, 74–103
Presidential Hotline 96
Presidential inauguration 104–7
Presidential powers 11–15, 23, 38–9
Presidential term of office 40
Primary elections 75–9, 81–2, 94–9, 185–94
Progressive Party 35, 43
Puerto Rico 33, 75
PUSH (People United to Save Humanity) 171–2

Race issues 48, 52, 54–5
Rafshoon, Gerald 83
Rather, Dan 158
Reagan, Nancy 85
Reagan, Ronald 38, 65, 70–3, 89, 94, 110, 111, 113, 115, 117, 120, 121, 124, 125, 131, 138, 140, 143, 145–6, 148, 150–2, 155, 156, 161–3, 166, 168, 175, 185, 196, 200
Reeve, Christopher 177
Regan, Donald 157, 168
Registration of voters 75
Regulation 39
Republican Party 17, 18, 20, 24–30, 32, 33, 34, 36–9, 42, 43, 45–7, 55, 57, 62, 65, 74, 77–9, 81, 82, 87–90, 96–9, 110, 111, 114, 117, 119, 124,

128, 143–9, 151, 154, 155, 157–9, 161, 162, 164–8, 185–98
Rhode Island 112–13
Rice, Donna 148, 178, 179, 180
Robb, Charles 184
Robertson, Pat 116, 145, 147–50, 152, 159–61, 164, 173, 187–92, 194
Ronstadt, Linda 85
Roosevelt, Franklin Delano 38–9, 40, 41, 54, 66, 90, 98, 110, 146
Roosevelt, Theodore 33–4, 36
Ruby, Jack 53
'Rustbelt' 112–13

Sadat, Anwar 68
Samoa 75, 127
Sandinista government 71, 72, 150–2
Scandals 27–8, 31, 36–7, 49, 62, 66, 70, 72, 85, 87, 92–3
Schroeder, Patricia 154, 184–5
Secret Service 81, 132
Segregation 48, 52
Selection procedures 22, 29–30, 75–80
Senate 13, 14, 16, 26, 73, 126–7, 130
Shah of Iran 68–9, 72
Sherman, John 30
Shriver, Sargent 50
Shultz, George 134, 156
'Silicon Valley' 119
Simon, Paul 144, 146, 147, 149, 152, 170, 176, 180–1, 187, 193
Slavery 25–6
Smith, Albert E. 38
Somoza, Anastasio 150
South Carolina 16, 20, 21, 29, 115–17
South Dakota 124–5, 176, 181, 189
Soviet Union 44, 47, 48, 51–2, 60–1, 65, 69, 73, 149, 158, 160, 166
Spain 20, 33
Spanish-American War 33
Speaker, Office of 127
Stalin, Josef 40, 166
Stanton, Edwin 26, 27
Star Wars 148–9, 172, 177
State Department 132
State government 138–41
State of the Union address 104, 153
States' Rights Democrats 43, 99, 111
Stennis, John 198
Stevenson, Adlai 45, 97

Strategic Defence Initiative (SDI) 148–9, 172, 177
Stuart, Gilbert 105
Suez 47, 48
'Sunbelt' 122–3
'Super Tuesday' 81, 83, 161, 164, 177, 181, 187
Supreme Court 25, 47, 73, 126, 135–7
Swaggart, Jimmy 148

Taft, William Howard 34–5, 46
Taft-Hartley Act 43
Taiwan 44
Tammany Hall 31
Taylor, Zachary 24, 27
Teapot Dome scandal 37
Television 49, 65, 90–2, 94–5, 160
Tennessee 20, 115–17, 168, 177
Tet offensive 56
Texas 53, 82, 118–19, 155, 170
Thatcher, Margaret 166
Third-party candidate 99
Thirteenth Amendment 25
Thomas, Tony 115
Thurmond, Strom 43, 99, 111
Tilden, Samuel 29
Time 158, 164, 179
Tippecanoe 23
Tonkin Gulf Resolution 55, 56
Tower Commission 156
Trade deficit 142–6
Transportation Department 133
Treasury Department 28, 132
Truman, Harry S. 40, 41–5, 87, 99, 111, 133–4, 175
TV-am 102
'Tweed, Boss' 28
Tyler, John 22–3, 24

Un-American Activities Committee 45, 47, 60, 131
Union, Act of 12–14, 19

United Nations 43, 44, 47
Utah 120–1

Vermont 112–13
Versailles Peace Conference 35
Veto, power of 14, 31
Vietnam War 46, 55–62, 63, 64, 77, 112
Virgin islands 75, 127
Virginia 115–17, 184
Voting machines 100
Voting Rights Act 75

Wall Street 38, 142–3
Wallace, George 52, 58, 61, 99
Wallace, Henry 43–4
War Powers resolution 64
Warsaw Pact 65
Washington, George 13, 14–15, 17, 18, 105
Washington Post 61, 155, 156
Washington State 120–1, 159
Watergate 61–2, 63, 65, 71, 87, 131, 165
Watts riots 55
Webster, Daniel 22
Weinberger, Casper 134, 156
Welfare 146–7
West Virginia 115–17
Westmoreland, Gen. 56
Whig Party 22–3, 24
'Whistle-stop' tour 90
White House 105–7
Wilkie, Wendell 90
Wilson, Harold 189
Wilson, James 11
Wilson, Woodrow 35–6
Wisconsin 34, 75, 113–15, 170, 192
Women, votes for 36, 74
World Bank 43
World War One 35
World War Two 39–42, 44, 49
Wyoming 120–1

Yalta peace conference 40